Cook–A–Book

*A Cookbook of Delicious Reading
Enhancement Activities*
for Grades Pre–K to 6

&. &. &.

by Leslie Cefali

Copyright © 1991 Alleyside Press
All Rights Reserved
Published by Alleyside Press, A Division of Freline, Inc.
P. O. Box 889
Hagerstown, Maryland 21741

ISBN 0–913853–16–X

Printed in the United States of America

Table of Contents

Introduction

The recipes in this book can be used at home or in the classroom to help children become involved with quality literature and reading. The books become a part of a child's life as the child makes the foods that are actually eaten in the book. When one boy in my class reminded me that we had to throw three kisses at the pasta pot before we took it off the heat, when we made pasta from scratch to extend the book *Strega Nona* by Tomie dePaola, I became aware that these activities helped the children "live" the story.

The importance of reading aloud to children is emphasized continually in educational research. The current study, *Becoming a Nation of Readers: The Report of the Commission on Reading*, by the National Academy of Education, The National Institute of Education, and The Center for the Study of Reading, states that the single most important activity for successful reading is reading aloud to children. Other current sources include the popular *Read-Aloud Handbook* by Jim Trelease, and the national television special entitled "Drop Everything and Read."

Cooking can be a great motivator in reading because the participants are totally immersed in language development, concept building, sequence skills, comprehension, and listening skills, resulting in a deeper involvement with books and literature. In addition to sharing quality literature through these recipes, cooking is important in a classroom because it covers the entire curriculum. Besides the language arts, it encompasses math, science, health, nutrition, and social studies. Cooking actively involves every child in a class or home regardless of his or her academic level.

Having cooking experiences that are centered around children's literature help make the books become "real" for children. Children need concrete learning experiences to get involved in the learning process. What better way for them to become a part of a book than to experience cooking and preparing food that is eaten in nursery rhymes and literature?

I have found that the books we use for cooking experiences are long remembered and cherished, even years later. These books are ones that the children will probably never forget.

> Books should not be viewed as ends in themselves but as windows that open through to new ideas and lead to

more investigation, study, and recreation. When your children become more than superficially interested in books they read, their reading interests broaden and they are more likely to maintain their reading habit than if they merely jump from one book to another *(Growing Up Reading,* Linda Leonard Lamme, Acropolis Books, 1985, p. 163).

Besides offering the children fun, concrete, and meaningful relationships with books, cooking with books also benefits the parents and other family members. I always send home a note listing the books and activities that we have done in class. Many children will later tell me that they have reread the book and have often prepared the food at home with their parents. Several parents at conferences have made comments about the book-related cooking experiences, and some have even called years later to ask about a book or activity that we had done when their child was in my class.

All foods included in this book are taken directly from quality literature. Many of the books have received awards for their contributions to children's literature. My students have made jam with Sal and her mother in *Blueberries for Sal* and have eaten Turkish Delight with Eustace in *The Lion, the Witch and the Wardrobe.*

Though we cook often in my classroom during first semester, I try to "cook-a-book" regularly every week during the second semester. We spend a lot of time during the first part of the year reading many books, both those that we will use in cooking and many that we will not. When we do "cook-a-book," I want my children to be familiar with the story already. I want the cooking activity to *further* their enjoyment of the book, not to be the sole reason for it. My main purpose in these cooking experiences is to promote the enjoyment of books and reading. By second semester, I also know which parents are able and willing to help with the cooking experiences and the children are settled into a routine without too many holiday interruptions.

Some of the recipes in this book take more time than others. On days when I am feeling rushed, or I do not want to bring in a lot of ingredients, I will use (for example) the recipe listed with *Bread and Jam for Frances* by Russell Hoban. The children simply spread grape jam on pieces of bread. For this activity I simply have a mother, father, or other helper call the children over to a table two or three at a time during the morning when I am working with small groups and individual students. The cooking experience does not need to take up any more time in your day. This arrangement works equally well when the children are cooking with an oven or electric skillet.

I generally have a class size of 28 to 30 students. The secret in cooking with students is to be sure everyone has a chance to do *something*. My students will wait patiently if they know that they will have an important role in the activity. Be sure to have the students, not the adults, do most of the work—stirring, cracking eggs, pouring, kneading, cutting. It is extremely important that the children help with even the smallest contribution. If you have 30 students, stir your batter 30 times.

When I first began teaching and cooking in my classroom, I would bring my ingredients and all my kitchen supplies the day we were cooking. Almost every time I would leave something important at home, such as the colander, a potholder, or even the pot! I now have a small cabinet at school to store all my supplies. Some of the kitchen utensils were extras I had at home; others were picked up at garage sales or secondhand stores, and still others were donated by parents. A note sent home explaining what you need donated is usually effective.

Here is a list of cooking supplies that I keep at school:

- plastic silverware (about 30 knives, forks and spoons)
- electric skillet
- 2 rectangular cake pans
- 2 square cake pans
- 1 cookie sheet
- 1 saucepan with lid
- 1 hot plate (an electrical appliance similar to a stove burner)
- 1 colander
- 4 metal mixing bowls, various sizes
- 1 popcorn popper (the older model that you can cook in)
- 1 potato masher
- 1 timer
- 3 or 4 sets of measuring spoons
- 2 or 3 sets of measuring cups, both dry and liquid
- 1 ladle
- 1 spatula
- several metal forks, knives and spoons
- 2 large cutting boards
- 3 wooden spoons
- 10 sharp knives
- 1 bottle opener
- 1 can opener
- 2 or 3 sets of dish cloths and towels
- 2 or 3 hot mats
- 35 plastic coffee cups
- several packages of paper cups
- napkins
- food coloring
- foil cupcake liners
- paper plates
- 1 small electric oven (We usually use the oven in the school kitchen when we have a lot to bake.)
- dish soap

Happy cooking—and most importantly, happy reading!

Recipes

Laughing Latkes

M. B. Goffstein
Farrar, Straus, and Giroux, 1980

Do *latkes* laugh when you eat them with sour cream? *Latkes* are a traditional Hanukkah meal. These potato pancakes are good to eat while celebrating the holidays in December, or anytime during the year.

Latkes

5 large potatoes
1 small onion
½ teaspoon baking powder
1 teaspoon salt
2 eggs
1½ tablespoons flour

Scrub the potatoes. Using a cheese grater, let the children grate the potatoes and onion. Mix in baking powder, salt, eggs, and flour. Using a tablespoon, pour batter into a hot greased electric skillet. Serve with sour cream or applesauce. Makes about 45 to 50 small *latkes*.

Tuck Everlasting

Natalie Babbitt
Farrar, Straus, and Giroux, 1975

Winnie Foster discovers a fascinating secret about Miles Tuck and his family and why they never seem to age. This book will spark an engaging discussion about the advantages and disadvantages of living forever. Winnie eats supper at the Tucks' home one evening when they have flapjacks, bacon, bread, and applesauce.

Flapjacks

3 eggs

2½ cups buttermilk

1 teaspoon baking powder

1 teaspoon baking soda

½ teaspoon salt

2–2½ cups flour

2 tablespoons oil

Beat eggs; add milk. Mix dry ingredients in separate bowl. Slowly add dry ingredients to milk-and-egg mixture. Add oil and mix well. Pour batter onto a hot greased skillet. When bubbles appear on pancakes, turn and cook until second side is golden brown. Serve warm with syrup.

To duplicate the Tucks' meal, also fry 1 piece of bacon per child. Serve bread and applesauce to complete the meal.

The Blueberry Bears

Eleanor Lapp
Illustrated by Margot Apple
Albert Whitman, 1983

Bessie Allen picked and picked the blueberries that grew behind her cabin. She froze them, canned them, made pies, muffins, and pancakes with them. You can enjoy the blueberry muffin recipe in the book or make some blueberry pancakes. Just be sure to leave some in the patch for the bears!

Blueberry Pancakes

1 egg, beaten

1 cup milk

2 tablespoons oil

1¼ cups flour

1 tablespoon sugar

3 teaspoons baking powder

½ teaspoon salt

blueberries

Combine egg, milk, and oil. Add dry ingredients; mix well. Pour batter into hot, greased skillet. When pancakes bubble, add blueberries to each pancake, turn and cook the other side until golden brown. Serve with butter and syrup.

The Pancake

Anita Lobel
Greenwillow, 1978

Here is yet another book based on the theme of runaway food. This time a pancake runs away from a woman, her seven children, her husband, and several farm animals. It is a pig in this book who finally catches the pancake and eats him. The woman takes the whole gang, including the animals, back home and makes another pancake and they all eat him before he gets away.

Pancakes

2 cups flour

4 teaspoons baking powder

2 tablespoons sugar

1 teaspoon salt

1½ cups milk

2 eggs, beaten

4 tablespoons melted butter

Sift the dry ingredients into a bowl. Blend milk, eggs, and butter in a separate bowl, then mix with the dry ingredients. Drop batter by the spoonful into a hot skillet. Turn when bubbles appear on the pancakes. Cook other side until golden brown.

Pancakes, Pancakes

Eric Carle
Alfred A. Knopf, 1970

Jack wants pancakes for breakfast and helps his mother make
them. He goes to the mill for the flour, to the henhouse for eggs,
to the meadow to milk the cow. He makes butter, gathers the
wood for the fire, and goes to the cellar for the homemade jam.
This story, like *Pancakes for Breakfast* by Tomie dePaola, shows
where many of our breakfast foods come from. Make as much
as you can from scratch. Recipes for all the foods are listed
elsewhere in this book. The recipe below is for pancakes. Eat
them with strawberry jam, as Jack does in the book.

Pancakes

¼ stick butter

2 cups milk

pinch of salt

2 eggs

⅓ cup sugar

1 cup flour

Melt butter and mix with milk, salt, eggs, and sugar. Add flour
and blend well. Cook pancakes in a very hot skillet. Serve with
butter and strawberry jam.

Journey Cake, Ho

Caldecott Honor Book

Ruth Sawyer
Illustrated by Robert McCloskey
Viking Press, 1953

This book is another version of the gingerbread man story. This time it is a journey cake or pancake that tries to escape from a parade of characters who want to eat him for dinner.

Journey Cake

1½ cups cornmeal

1 teaspoon baking powder

½ teaspoon salt

3 eggs

1 cup milk

1½ cups flour

1 tablespoon sugar

½ cup shortening

Sift together cornmeal, baking powder, and salt. Add eggs, beating well after adding each one. Add milk, shortening, and dry ingredients. Spoon batter onto a hot, greased skillet. Turn journey cakes when they start to bubble. Cook other side until brown. Serve with syrup—if they don't run away!

Johnny-Cake

Joseph Jacobs
G. P. Putnam, 1933

Johnny-Cake, like the gingerbread boy, pops out of the oven while he is being cooked. This is another one of many variations on this theme. When you make a johnny-cake, try to eat him before he escapes down the hallway!

Johnny-Cake

4 cups biscuit mix

2 eggs

2½ cups milk

butter

Mix the biscuit mix and eggs. Gradually add milk and mix until smooth. Add more milk if the batter needs to be a bit thinner. Melt butter in skillet. Pour batter making 2–3″ pancakes. Turn pancakes when bubbles appear. Cook other side until brown. Serve warm with butter and syrup or jam.

If I Could Be My Grandmother

Steven Kroll
Illustrated by Lady McCrady
Pantheon, 1977

What would you do if you were a grandmother? The little girl in this book role-plays all the things she would do. She would bake cookies and have cornflakes for breakfast. Find out what your students would do if they were grandparents.

Cornflakes

Bring a large box of cornflakes, and some milk and sugar to school. Each child can prepare his or her own bowl of cereal.

Cookies

1 pkg. cake mix, any flavor   *½ cup cooking oil*
2 eggs   *2 tablespoons water*

Combine ingredients and mix well. Drop batter by the spoonful onto a greased cookie sheet. Bake for 9 minutes at 350°.

≥a ≥a ≥a

The Cereal Box

David McPhail
Little, Brown and Co., 1974

Breakfast in this household is a real adventure. Everyone eats a different kind of cereal. The one the little boy eats is in a green box and it seems to contain more than just cereal! There's a pair of glasses, a live frog, a bird, and other surprises. There's even a creature with one eye!

Cereal

Bring in some dry cereal that is packaged in a green box. Or ask your students to bring in cereal that comes in a green box and see how many different kinds of cereal you get. Bring out the bowls, milk, and sugar and let your children choose the kind of cereal they would like to eat. Be sure to check the gifts included in the cereal boxes to see if you can find a monster with one eye!

ð& ð& ð&

Goldilocks and the Three Bears

Retold and illustrated by Jan Brett
Dodd, Mead, and Co., 1987

Jan Brett does a beautiful rendition of this classic fairy tale. This version is not to be missed!

Porridge

For each child you will need:

¾ cup water	*raisins*
⅛ teaspoon salt	*brown sugar*
⅓ cup old-fashioned rolled oats	*milk*

Bring the water to a boil. Add salt and oats. Cook for 5 minutes, stirring occasionally. Let stand a few minutes to thicken before serving. Add raisins, brown sugar, and milk if desired.

The Magic Porridge Pot

Traditional Folk Tale

A little girl and her widowed mother are given a magic pot. The pot starts and stops cooking porridge on command, with some magic words. One day when the little girl is gone, her mother prepares some porridge. The mother forgets the magic words to turn off the pot. Before long, porridge flows from her house and out onto the streets of the town. Will the magic pot ever stop making porridge? You might want to read this story and have your students compare it with Tomie dePaola's book *Strega Nona*.

Porridge

For each child you will need:

1 cup water

⅛ teaspoon salt

⅓ cup oat bran cereal

Mix the ingredients. Heat to a boil, stirring constantly. Reduce to low heat and cook for 1 to 2 minutes. Serve with brown sugar, cinnamon, raisins, or apple pieces if desired.

Pease Porridge Hot

Traditional Mother Goose

Pease porridge hot.
Pease porridge cold.
Pease porridge in a pot
Nine days old.

Some like it hot,
Some like it cold.
Some like it in a pot
Nine days old.

Porridge

For each child you will need:

¾ cup water

⅛ teaspoon salt

2½ tablespoons instant hot cereal

Heat water and salt until water just starts to boil. Stir in cereal. Cook 30 seconds. Remove from heat and let stand about 1 minute. For a creamier consistency, use milk instead of water.

Journey to America

Sonia Levitin
Atheneum, 1970

The Nazis are moving into Germany and Lisa Platt's father has to leave for America. Lisa, her mother, and two sisters move to Switzerland to wait for their father to send for them. The hardships of the war are shared in this historical fiction book.

The only food many of the people had to eat was oatmeal—for breakfast, lunch, and dinner. One evening, all Lisa ate was oatmeal, crackers, and a half an apple. Another meal consisted of oatmeal and beans. Cook these meals in class to allow your children to imagine what meals were like during Hitler's dictatorship.

Oatmeal

For each child you will need:

¾ cup water

⅛ teaspoon salt

⅓ cup old-fashioned rolled oats

Bring water to a boil. Add salt and oatmeal. Cook for 5 minutes, stirring constantly. Let stand a few minutes to thicken before serving. Serve with half an apple.

How My Parents Learned to Eat

Reading Rainbow Selection

Ina R. Friedman
Illustrated by Allen Say
Houghton Mifflin Co., 1984

When an American sailor and a Japanese woman marry, their daughter learns to eat both with a fork and with chopsticks.

Prepare rice with your students and teach them how to use chopsticks. Wooden chopsticks can be purchased very inexpensively and the children can each have their pair to use and take home.

White Rice

1 cup white rice

2 cups water

1 tablespoon oil or butter

Combine the rice, water, and butter in a 1 quart pan. Bring to a boil. Cover pan with lid. Turn heat down to low and simmer for 20 minutes.

The Funny Little Woman

Caldecott Award Winner

Retold by Arlene Mosel
Illustrated by Blair Lent
E. P. Dutton, 1972

The funny little woman makes a rice dumpling that falls down a hole in the ground to a strange underworld and the home of the wicked *oni*. Will she be able to escape from him?

Rice Dumplings

1 cup flour

2 teaspoons baking powder

¼ teaspoon salt

2 tablespoons oil

½ cup milk

1 cup white rice, cooked

1 can chicken broth

Combine the dry ingredients, then mix oil, milk and rice. Heat chicken broth in a pot. Place dumplings into boiling chicken broth. Cover and cook 15 minutes. Do not lift the cover while dumplings are steaming.

Davy Dumpling

Traditional Mother Goose

Davy Davy Dumpling,
Boil him in a pot;
Sugar him and butter him,
Eat him while he's hot.

Dumplings

2 cups flour

3½ teaspoons baking powder

½ cup milk

½ teaspoon salt

2 cans chicken broth

Combine flour, baking powder, milk, and salt; mix well. Heat the chicken broth until it boils. Turn down to medium heat. Drop dumplings by the spoonful into broth. Turn heat down to medium. Put lid on pot and cook dumplings for 15 minutes.

Strega Nona

Caldecott Honor Book

Tomie dePaola
Prentice Hall, 1975

Strega Nona owns a magic pasta pot and warns her helper, Big Anthony, never to touch it. One day when Strega Nona goes out to visit her friend, Big Anthony disobeys Strega Nona and tries to make pasta with the magic pot. When Strega Nona returns, she knows what has happened as pasta has overflowed from the pot and is covering the town. How does all this pasta get cleaned up in time for Strega Nona to sleep in her bed that night?

Homemade Pasta

1½ cups flour
½ teaspoon salt
2 eggs, beaten
1 stick margarine
4 oz. can Parmesan cheese

Combine flour, salt, and eggs. On a lightly floured cutting board, let the children roll out the dough until it is thin. Allow each child to cut noodles into strips with a knife. Let the children break the noodles until they are approximately 3" long. Place noodles into boiling water and cook until tender. Drain. Mix in the margarine and can of cheese.

Have one adult with each group of eight to ten children making this recipe. Cook all pasta together in a large pot. A pasta machine can be used, but the children participate more if they have to roll the dough themselves.

Spaghetti Eddie

Mary Ellis
T. S. Denison, 1957

Eddie and his sister, Joan, make spaghetti for dinner to surprise their mother when she comes home from work. Eddie insists that more spaghetti is needed and convinces a delivery man to add more to the pot when he comes to deliver groceries. When they end up with more spaghetti than they can eat, Eddie delivers bowls of pasta to neighbors and friends. Make enough spaghetti so your students can deliver some to the teachers, secretary, principal, and other friends at school.

Spaghetti

1 lb. hamburger

1 pkg. spaghetti seasonings

6 oz. can tomato paste

1¼ cups water

Brown the hamburger in a skillet. Drain off grease. Add the seasonings, tomato paste, and water. Simmer about 30 minutes. Prepare spaghetti noodles. Serve hot with Parmesan cheese.

Curious George Takes a Job

H. A. Rey
Scholastic Book Services, 1947

When Curious George's curiosity gets the better of him, he wants to know what is going on outside the zoo. He escapes and one of the first places he discovers is the kitchen of a restaurant, where he finds spaghetti cooking on the stove.

When you cook this spaghetti, watch out for curious monkeys!

Spaghetti

Follow the directions on the box to prepare one pound of spaghetti. In the book, George eats the noodles right from the pot, with no sauce. Your students might want to try it this way, or with butter and a sprinkle of garlic powder and Parmesan cheese.

Little Nino's Pizzeria

Reading Rainbow Selection

Karen Barbour
Harcourt Brace Jovanovich, 1987

When Nino the pizza maker closes his family-run pizzeria, Little Nino's, and opens up a big, fancy, expensive restaurant called Big Nino's, he finds the paperwork and the money talk has taken over what he really wants to do—make pizza! This book can be enjoyed as a story, as well as an introduction to comparing small businesses and large businesses.

Pizza

1 pkg. hot roll mix
1½ cups hot water
2 tablespoons cooking oil
cornmeal
8 oz. can pizza sauce
oregano

mozzarella cheese
cooked hamburger or
*   pepperoni*
onions, finely chopped
green pepper, diced

Combine hot roll mix, hot water, and oil. Mix well. Let the children take turns kneading the dough for about 5 minutes. Give each child a piece of dough about the size of a golf ball and a small square of greased aluminum foil. Have the children sprinkle a small amount of cornmeal onto the foil and flatten their dough into a circle, forming their pizza crust. Allow the children to spoon a small amount of pizza sauce and other toppings onto their mini pizzas. Place their pizzas on the foil onto cookie sheets. You can write their names on the foil with a permanent marker. Bake in a 425° oven for 12 to 15 minutes.

Curious George and the Pizza

Margaret and H. A. Rey
Scholastic Book Services, 1985

As usual, George's curiosity gets him into some comical troubles. This time George finds himself in a pizza parlor. Sometimes local pizza parlors will allow you to take your class in to make their own individual pizzas. Or you might choose to make pizza at school. If you want your children to experience kneading their own crust, see the recipe included for the book *Little Nino's Pizzeria* on page 25.

Pizza

2 frozen pizza crusts

2 cans pizza or tomato sauce

cooked hamburger, pepperoni, or sausage

onions, green peppers, mushrooms, if desired

1½–2 lbs. mozzarella cheese

The students can take turns grating the cheese. Place the crusts onto two pizza pans, and add tomato sauce and desired toppings. Bake at 400° for 8 to 9 minutes or until the cheese starts to brown.

An Early American Christmas

Tomie dePaola
Holiday House, 1987

This book tells what Christmas was like during colonial times. There are many Christmas foods and activities that you can make and do after enjoying this book. If you want to string popcorn for your Christmas tree, pop it one day and string it the next, as the book suggests. Popcorn is much easier to string if it sits out for a day. Perhaps you will want to cook up some pretzels.

Pretzels

1 pkg. quick-rise dry yeast

¾ cup warm water

1½ teaspoons salt

1 tablespoon sugar

1½–3 cups flour

egg white

coarse salt

Combine water and yeast. When the yeast is dissolved, add the salt and sugar. Mix in 2 cups of flour. Add more flour if needed until the dough loses its stickiness. Knead dough until smooth (about 5 to 10 minutes). Let dough rise 30 to 40 minutes.

After the dough rises, give each child a piece about the size of a 2" ball. Roll into a rope and twist into pretzel shape. Place on greased cookie sheet. Brush with egg white and sprinkle with coarse salt. Bake 12 to 15 minutes in a 425° oven.

Cranberry Thanksgiving

Wende and Harry Devlin
Parents' Magazine Press, 1971

When Maggie and her grandmother have company for Thanksgiving Dinner, Grandmother's famous cranberry bread recipe disappears. Who would have taken it? Included in the book is Grandmother's Famous Cranberry Bread Recipe. It is such a guarded secret that you'll have to read the book to find out what it is! Included below is a recipe for a not-so-famous but still delicious cranberry bread.

Cranberry Bread

2 cups flour

½ teaspoon salt

2 teaspoons baking powder

½ teaspoon baking soda

1 cup sugar

⅛ teaspoon cinnamon

1 egg, beaten

2 tablespoons oil

2 tablespoons hot water

¼ cup grated orange rind

½ cup orange juice

1 cup cut cranberries

½ cup chopped nuts

Mix flour, salt, baking powder, baking soda, sugar, and cinnamon. In a separate bowl, blend egg, oil, water, orange rind, and orange juice. Stir this mixture into dry ingredients. Add cranberries and nuts. Pour into two greased loaf pans. Bake for 1 hour and 10 minutes at 325°.

The Sign of the Beaver

Newbery Honor Book

Elizabeth George Speare
Houghton Mifflin, 1983

Twelve-year-old Matt is left alone in the Maine wilderness in his family's cabin to wait for his father's return. Matt must learn to survive on his own, to find food and to protect himself from wild animals, strangers, and Indians. When he meets an Indian chief and his grandson, Attean, Matt learns a lot about survival in the wilderness.

Many months pass and there is no sign of Matt's family. Matt needs to decide whether to move on with Attean and his family, who have by now become like family to him, or to continue to wait for his own family, from whom he has not heard.

Corn Cake

1¼ cups flour
¾ cup corn meal
2 tablespoons sugar
4 teaspoons baking powder
½ teaspoon baking soda

1 teaspoon salt
1 cup milk
4 tablespoons oil
2 eggs

Mix dry ingredients. In a separate bowl, combine milk, oil, eggs; mix well. Add milk mixture to dry ingredients; stir well. Pour batter in greased 8" pan. Bake for 20 to 25 minutes in a 425° oven. Serve with molasses to enjoy the corn cake just as Matt did in this book.

The Giant Jam Sandwich

John Vernon Lord
Houghton Mifflin, 1972

When four million wasps fly into Itching Down, the residents do all they can to get rid of them. They finally decide to make a giant jam sandwich. They bake the bread and bring in strawberry jam by the truckload.

At some delicatessens you can order fresh bread as long as five feet or longer! If you can order such a loaf, your students would enjoy spreading strawberry jam on it. If you would like to bake your own bread—not quite so large—this is a batter bread that does not have to be kneaded.

Bread

2¾–3½ cups flour   *2 tablespoons oil*

1½ teaspoons salt   *1½ cup very hot water*

½ cup wheat germ   *2 tablespoons molasses*

2 pkg. quick-rise yeast

Mix 1 cup flour with salt, wheat germ, and yeast. Add oil. Gradually add water and molasses to flour mixture and beat 3 minutes at medium speed with an electric mixer. Add ½ cup flour. Beat at high speed. Add enough flour to make a stiff batter. Cover and let rise in a warm, draft-free place until dough doubles—about 30 minutes.

Stir down batter. Beat for about 30 seconds. Turn into a greased 1½ quart casserole dish. Let rise again about 30 minutes. Bake at 375° about 45 minutes. Remove from casserole dish and cool.

The Little Red Hen

Traditional Fairy Tale

The little red hen plants the wheat, harvests the wheat, takes it to the mill to be ground into flour, and then bakes the bread. When she asks her friends to help, none of them will—that is, until they want to help her eat the bread!

Arrange a trip to a flour mill or bakery, if possible. Your class will willingly help bake this bread!

Whole Wheat Bread

2 cups milk, scalded

2 tablespoons oil

2 tablespoons honey

1 tablespoon molasses

2 teaspoons salt

1 pkg. quick-rise yeast

¼ cup warm water

about 5½ cups whole wheat flour

Combine milk, oil, honey, molasses, and salt. Mix well and cool to lukewarm. Dissolve yeast in water. Stir into mixture. Gradually add flour to make a stiff dough. Beat well each time you add more flour. Cover with damp towel. Put in a warm, draft-free area. Let dough rise until it is doubled. Punch down and knead on a floured surface until it is smooth and elastic-like. Divide dough in half and place in greased breadpans. Brush with melted butter. Cover and let rise until doubled in size again. Bake at 375° for 40 to 45 minutes. Remove from pans and cool.

The Clever Hen

Traditional Mother Goose

I had a little hen, the prettiest ever seen;
She washed me the dishes and she kept the house clean.
She went to the mill to fetch me some flour;
She brought it home in less than an hour.
She baked me my bread, she brewed me my ale,
She sat by the fire and told many a fine tale.

Bread

If you want to bake bread from scratch, see the recipe listed with the book *The Little Red Hen* on page 31 or *The Giant Jam Sandwich* on page 30.

Another alternative is to buy frozen bread at the grocery store. Thaw the bread overnight in the refrigerator, or for 2 hours at room temperature. Place the thawed dough in greased loaf pans. Let rise in a draft-free area until the bread rises 1" over the top of the pans. Bake for 25 to 35 minutes at 350°.

ða ða ða

Little Tommy Tucker

Traditional Mother Goose

Little Tommy Tucker
Sings for his supper.
What shall we give him?
White bread and butter

Bread and Butter

Buy 1 or 2 loaves of white bread and a tub of butter (not margarine). Allow the children to butter their own pieces of bread. If you are talking about shapes, let them cut their bread into two rectangles or triangles. This is also a good way to teach them about the concept "one-half."

You might want to provide both salted and unsalted butter so your students can taste the difference between the two. If you want to make your own butter, see the recipe listed under *Pancakes for Breakfast* (page 34). To make your own bread, see the bread recipe with *The Little Red Hen* on page 31.

ò. ò. ò.

Little Red Riding Hood

Caldecott Honor Book

*Retold and illustrated by Trina Schart Hyman
Holiday House, 1983*

In this beautifully illustrated version of the well-known fairy tale, Little Red Riding Hood takes sweet butter, bread, and wine to grandmother's house.

Bread and Sweet Butter

Let each child butter his or her own piece of bread to eat after reading this book together. If you do not want to use store-bought bread and butter, you can find the recipe for butter under *Pancakes for Breakfast* on page 34, and the recipe for homemade bread under *The Little Red Hen* on page 31.

Pancakes for Breakfast

Tomie dePaola
Harcourt Brace Jovanovich, 1978

Included in this wordless book is a recipe for pancakes. In addition to making pancakes, the little old lady goes to the chicken house to fetch her eggs, milks the cow to make butter, churns her butter, and purchases maple syrup from a man who taps his own trees.

If you can arrange to visit a farm to buy eggs and milk or go to a maple sugaring, it would really help your students to live the experiences in this book. Be sure to make pancakes from the recipe in the book and serve them up with some homemade butter.

Homemade Butter

2 cartons heavy cream

5–6 jars with lids; baby food jars work well

Evenly divide the 2 cartons of cream in the jars. Have your students sit in a circle and distribute the jars to every fifth or sixth child. Let each student shake the jar 50 or 60 times before passing it to the next child. If you sing a song and pass the jars after the song each time, the task will pass more quickly. It takes about 20 to 40 minutes, depending on the temperature and age of the cream, before the butter separates from the buttermilk. If you use several jars as suggested, the children will get a chance to shake the jar more often than if you just use one jar.

Salt the butter slightly before serving if desired. Use the butter on pancakes, as in the book, or spread it on saltine crackers. (See the recipe for pancakes listed with the book *Johnny-Cake* on page 13.)

You might want to point out the difference in color between homemade butter and store-bought. You can add some yellow food coloring to point out that the color does not change the taste.

ce ce ce

Bread and Jam for Frances

Russell Hoban
Illustrated by Lillian Hoban
Harper and Row, 1964

Frances does not want to eat anything but bread and jam for breakfast, lunch, and dinner. Her family tries to get her to try some other foods but to no avail. How do her parents finally solve this problem?

Bread and Jam

1 to 2 loaves of bread
1 jar grape jam

Each child spreads about a tablespoon of jam on his or her bread. This can be eaten as an open-face sandwich, or the child can use 2 pieces of bread for a jam sandwich.

A Bear Called Paddington

Michael Bond
Dell, 1968

In the Paddington Bear series, Paddington has a real fondness for marmalade.

Marmalade

3 oranges

2 lemons

10 cups water

8 cups sugar

Thoroughly wash the rind on all fruit. Cut into quarters, remove seeds, and soak in 10 cups of water overnight. Remove fruit from water and reserve water. Cut oranges and lemons into fine pieces. Put fruit pieces back in water and boil for 1 hour. Add sugar. Boil until a candy thermometer reaches 222°. Pour into sterilized baby food jars.

Jamberry

Bruce Degen
Harper and Row, 1983

This book is written in rhyme, celebrating a variety of berries—
raspberries, blueberries, strawberries, and even a brassberry
band. You can't help but want to make jam!

Strawberry Jam

2 pints strawberries

4 cups sugar

3 oz. liquid fruit pectin

2 tablespoons lemon juice

Using a potato masher, mash 1 pint of strawberries at a time
until you have 2 cups of mashed berries. Add sugar and mix
well. Let stand 10 minutes. In another bowl, mix lemon juice
and liquid pectin. Add this to the strawberries. Stir for 3 to 4
minutes, mixing well. Fill sterilized baby food jars. Let jam set
for 24 hours at room temperature. Store in refrigerator
or freezer.

Blueberries for Sal

Caldecott Honor Book

Robert McCloskey
Viking Press, 1948

If possible, take your class blueberry-picking before making blueberry jam just like Little Sal and her mother.

Blueberry Jam

3 pints blueberries

3 tablespoons lemon juice

7 cups sugar

2 pouches liquid fruit pectin

Wash berries and remove stems. Using a potato masher, crush berries in a large bowl. Measure 4½ cups mashed berries. If you do not have 4½ cups, add water until you have this amount.

Combine blueberries and lemon juice in a cooking pot. Stir in sugar. Bring to a full rolling boil. Boil for 1 minute, stirring constantly. Remove from heat. Stir in pectin. Skim off foam. Put into sterilized baby food jars.

Jam Day

Barbara M. Josse
Illustrated by Emily Arnold McCully
Harper and Row, 1987

Early one morning when Ben and his mother are visiting Grandma and Grandpap, Grandma announces that it is Jam Day! The family goes strawberry-picking and returns to make jam and Grandpap's world-famous biscuit recipe. There is a recipe for strawberry jam listed for the book *Jamberry* on page 37.

Biscuits

2 cups flour

4 teaspoons baking powder

½ teaspoon salt

2 tablespoons sugar

½ teaspoon cream of tartar

½ cup shortening

⅔ cup milk

1 egg, unbeaten

Sift flour, baking powder, salt, sugar, and cream of tartar into a bowl. Add shortening and blend until it has a cornmeal-like consistency. Slowly pour milk into the flour mixture. Add egg and stir to a stiff dough. Knead 5 times. Roll dough to ½" thickness. Cut with 1½"cookie cutter. Bake for 10 to 15 minutes at 450°.

Hot Cross Buns

Traditional Mother Goose

Hot cross buns, hot cross buns,
One a penny, two a penny,
Hot cross buns.
Give them to your daughters,
Give them to your sons;
One a penny, two a penny,
Hot cross buns.

Hot Cross Buns

3½–4 cups flour	*½ teaspoon salt*
2 pkgs. quick-rise yeast	*3 eggs*
2 teaspoons cinnamon	*⅔ cup raisins*
½ cup oil	*1 egg white, beaten*
¾ cup milk	*frosting*
⅓ cup sugar	

Combine 2 cups of the flour with yeast and cinnamon. Heat oil, milk, sugar, and salt until it is 115° on a candy thermometer. Add the milk mixture to the dry ingredients. Add eggs and beat at a low speed with an electric beater for about 1 minute. Stir in the raisins. Add enough flour to make a soft dough. Place into a greased bowl; cover and let rise until dough doubles. Punch down, cover, and let rise 5 to 10 more minutes.

Divide dough into 16 balls. Put on greased cookie sheet about 1½" apart. Cover and let rise again until doubled. With a knife, cut an "X" or cross on each bun. Brush each bun with beaten egg white. Bake for 12 to 15 minutes in a 375° oven. Using a tube of frosting, frost an X or cross on each bun.

The Bun

Marcia Brown
Harcourt Brace Jovanovich, 1972

This Russian tale is another of the many books that utilize the theme of the *Gingerbread Man*. A little old woman makes a bun for a little old man. When the bun is set in the window, he begins to roll away. He is chased by the little old man and woman and several animals until, like the gingerbread man, he is tricked by the sly old fox.

Buns

4 cups self-rising flour

¼ cup sugar

1 pkg. yeast

1 egg, well beaten

¾ stick melted butter

2 cups warm water

Mix all ingredients together. Grease muffin tins and fill them half full. Let rise. Bake for 20 minutes at 375°. Makes about 30 buns.

The Muffin Man

Traditional Mother Goose

Oh, do you know the muffin man,
The muffin man, the muffin man?
Oh, do you know the muffin man
Who lives on Drury Lane?

Muffins

2 cups biscuit mix

2 tablespoons sugar

1 egg

¾ cup milk

Combine the above ingredients and beat vigorously for half a minute. Grease muffin tins. Fill tins ⅔ full. Bake in a 400° oven for 15 minutes.

Topping

1 cup sugar

1 teaspoon cinnamon

1 stick butter or margarine

Combine sugar and cinnamon. Melt butter. When muffins are done, dip the top in the melted butter and roll in sugar mixture.

Loose Tooth

Steven Kroll
Illustrated by Tricia Tusa
Holiday House, 1984

Flapper and Fangs are twin bats and do everything together until Fang loses a tooth. Flapper feels like everyone now ignores him. He steals Fang's tooth and accidentally drops it in some muffin batter that Mom is making.

When you bake these muffins, you might want to put a peanut in the batter. The children will have to chew carefully until the peanut is found!

Muffins

1¼ cups flour
1 tablespoon baking powder
1¼ teaspoons salt
2 tablespoons sugar
1 cup bran cereal

1 cup milk
3 tablespoons cooking oil
1 egg
1 large peanut

Stir together the flour, baking powder, salt, and sugar. In a separate bowl, combine the cereal and milk; let stand for about 2 minutes. Add oil and egg; beat well. Add the dry ingredients and peanut to the egg mixture and stir only until combined. Do not over-stir. Pour batter into greased muffin cups or muffin papers until ⅔ full. Bake 20 to 25 minutes at 400°. Makes about 12 regular size muffins.

Molly and Grandpa

Sally G. Ward
Scholastic, 1986

As Grandpa looks for the recipe for blueberry muffins, Molly goes in the kitchen to get started. What is taking Grandpa so long? Molly starts without him. Wait until you see what happens in the kitchen!

You can buy a box of blueberry muffins where you find the cake mixes or you can use the easy recipe below.

Blueberry Muffins

2 cups flour

¼ cup sugar

½ teaspoon salt

1 tablespoon baking powder

1 cup milk

¼ cup cooking oil

2 eggs, lightly beaten

1 cup blueberries

Combine the dry ingredients. Mix in enough milk to make a stiff dough—you might not use the entire cup. Stir in the oil, eggs, and blueberries. Fill muffin cups ⅔ full. If you do not use cupcake paper, be sure to grease the muffin trays. Bake at 400° for 30 minutes. Makes approximately 1 dozen average size muffins or 2 dozen small muffins.

In the Night Kitchen

Caldecott Honor Book

Maurice Sendak
Harper and Row, 1970

In the night kitchen there are all kinds of strange things happening. Mickey awakens and goes to the kitchen, only to find himself in all sorts of adventures. Now, "thanks to Mickey we have cake every morning."

Morning Coffee Cake

1 cup margarine
1 cup sugar
2 eggs
2 teaspoons vanilla
1 teaspoon baking soda
1½ teaspoons baking powder
½ teaspoon salt
2 cups flour
1 cup sour cream

Cream margarine and sugar. Add eggs and vanilla. Beat thoroughly. Add sifted dry ingredients and sour cream alternating in thirds. Spread half of the batter in a greased 9x12" pan. Sprinkle half of the filling and topping mixture on top of the batter. Spread on remaining batter and sprinkle remaining filling and topping mixture on top of batter. Bake for 35 minutes at 350°.

Filling and topping:

⅓ cup brown sugar
1 cup chopped nuts
¼ cup sugar
2 teaspoons cinnamon

In a separate bowl, mix brown sugar, nuts, sugar, and cinnamon for filling and topping.

Homer Price

Robert McCloskey
Viking, 1943

Homer Price has many humorous adventures, the most famous being the chapter entitled "Doughnuts."

Doughnuts

refrigerator biscuits

cooking oil

powdered sugar

Using a bottle cap or thimble, let the students cut a hole from the center of a biscuit. Heat 1" of oil in electric skillet set at 350°. An adult should fry the doughnuts because of the extremely hot oil. Fry biscuits and cut-out holes in the oil about 1 minute on each side, or until browned. As you fry the doughnuts, add more oil as needed. Drain oil from doughnuts by placing them on paper towels. Roll in powdered sugar or eat them plain.

❦ ❦ ❦

Old Witch Rescues Halloween

Wende and Harry Devlin
Four Winds Press, 1972

Mean old Mr. Butterbean always chases children, and he has decided there will be no Halloween. Since he owns most of the town of Oldswick, Nicky knows the townspeople usually listen to whatever Mr. Butterbean says! Nicky calls on Old Witch to help. Will she be able to save Halloween this year?

Sugar Doughnuts

After reading this book, serve sugar doughnuts and apple cider like the children have at the party. If your class would like to make doughnuts, refer to the recipe listed with the book *Homer Price* on page 46.

ॐ ॐ ॐ

Queen of Hearts

Traditional Mother Goose

The queen of hearts,
She made some tarts,
All on a summer's day.
The knave of hearts,
He stole those tarts
And took them clean away.

Queen of Hearts Tarts

refrigerator biscuits

strawberry jelly

For each child you will need 2 biscuits and ½ teaspoon jelly. Using a heart-shaped cookie cutter, let the children cut out 2 hearts from the biscuits. Put ½ teaspoon strawberry jelly between the biscuits. Seal the biscuits together using fork tines. Bake as directed on the biscuit package.

Apple Pigs

Ruth Orbach
Philomel Books, 1981

What would you do if your apple tree produced more apples than you knew what to do with? The girl in this book makes a lot of apple dishes and apple pigs. Directions are given in the book for apple pigs. The recipe for one of the many treats mentioned in the book is given below.

Apple Pan Dowdy

4 cups cooking apples

¾ cup brown sugar, firmly packed

½ cup oatmeal

¾ teaspoon cinnamon

½ cup flour

⅓ cup butter

¼ teaspoon allspice

Let the children wash, peel, and slice the apples. Place them into an 8x8" greased cake pan. Combine remaining ingredients until crumbly. Evenly spread mixture over the apples. Bake at 350° for 30 to 40 minutes or until top is brown. Serve warm with whipped cream or ice cream.

Little Jack Horner

Traditional Mother Goose

Little Jack Horner sat in a corner
Eating his Christmas pie
He put in his thumb and pulled out a plum
And said, "What a good boy am I!"

Jack's Christmas Pie

½ cup brown sugar

½ cup flour

1 teaspoon cinnamon

¼ teaspoon allspice

4 cups fresh plums, sliced

2 tablespoons lemon juice

2 tablespoons margarine

two 9" pie crusts

Combine sugar, flour, and spices. Add plums and lemon juice; mix well. Put this mixture into pie crust and top with margarine. Put top pie crust over all and seal with fork tines. Cut slits in top pie crust. Bake at 425° for 30 minutes, or until juice bubbles through slits and the top is golden brown.

Three Little Kittens

Traditional Mother Goose

Three little kittens they lost their mittens.
And they began to cry,
"Oh Mother dear, we sadly fear
Our mittens we have lost."
"What! Lost your mittens, you naughty kittens!
Then you shall have no pie."
"Meow! Meow! Meow! Meow!
No, you shall have no pie."

Chocolate Cream Pie

4 ozs. chocolate chips

⅓ cup milk

2 tablespoons sugar

1 small pkg. cream cheese

3½ cups non-dairy frozen whipped topping

1 graham cracker pie crust

Heat chocolate and 2 tablespoons of the milk on low heat. Cream sugar and cream cheese together. Add remaining milk and melted chocolate. Beat until smooth. Fold in whipped topping. Put this mixture into the pie crust and freeze until firm.

The Adventures of Simple Simon

Retold and Illustrated by Chris Conover
Farrar, Straus, Giroux, 1987

This is a picture book of the long version of the traditional Mother Goose rhyme "Simple Simon." The pictures are beautiful and you will have fun finding other Mother Goose characters included in the pictures.

Simple Simon

For each child you will need:

1 graham cracker square

1 tablespoon butter or margarine

1 Ziploc plastic bag

1 foil cupcake liner

½ teaspoon sugar

1 tablespoon cherry pie filling

1 tablespoon whipped cream

Place graham cracker, butter, and sugar in Ziploc bag. Let children crush and mix the ingredients together. Press mixture into foil cupcake liner. Top with cherry pie filling and whipped cream.

Over the River
and Through the Woods

Lydia Maria Child
Illustrated by Brinton Turkle
Scholastic Book Services, 1974

This is a picture book version of the Thanksgiving song of the same name. If you are really ambitious, you can cook a small turkey or turkey breast after reading this book and singing this song. Or you can make the pumpkin pie mentioned in the book.

Individual Pumpkin Pies

Pie crust

For each child you will need:

2 graham crackers   *1 plastic sandwich bag*

1 teaspoon brown sugar   *1 muffin cup (foil)*

1 tablespoon corn oil

Place crackers, sugar, and oil in the plastic bag. Each child crushes the ingredients in the bag, mixing well. Press the crust into the foil muffin cup. Mix the following pie filling to put into the individual crusts:

Pumpkin pie filling

2 cans pumpkin

1 teaspoon allspice

2 teaspoons cinnamon

two 1 lb. bags mini-marshmallows

2 cartons non-dairy whipped topping

Combine all ingredients, except topping, and cook slowly until marshmallows are melted. In a separate bowl, beat topping, then combine with pumpkin mixture. Let each child fill his or her pie crust. Top with extra whipped topping.

ea ea ea

Nobody Stole the Pie

Sonia Levitin
Illustrated by Fernando Krahn
Harcourt Brace Jovanovich, 1980

In the center of town is a lollyberry tree. The townspeople made a giant pie from the lollyberries. Little by little the people and animals in town taste the pie until one day it has been eaten up. They call a town meeting to find out who stole the pie. They soon discover that no one person had taken the pie but that everyone helped to make it disappear.

Can't find lollyberries? Substitute cherries.

"Lollyberry" Pie

2 large pkgs. cream cheese
1 cup powdered sugar
16 oz. frozen non-dairy whipped topping
1 graham cracker crust
1 large can cherry pie filling

Mix together cream cheese, sugar, and whipped topping. Put this mixture into graham cracker crust. Top with cherry pie filling. Chill.

Bat, Bat, Come Under My Hat

Traditional Mother Goose

Bat, bat, come under my hat
And I'll give you a slice of bacon;
And when I bake, I'll give you cake
If I am not mistaken.

Raspberry Cake

4 eggs

1 pkg. white cake mix

10 oz. pkg. frozen red raspberries, thawed

1 pkg. raspberry gelatin

⅔ cup oil

2 teaspoons raspberry flavoring, if available

Combine all ingredients in a large bowl. Mix well. Spread in a well-greased 13x9" baking pan. Bake in a 325° oven for 50 minutes, or until done. Top with whipped cream.

Pat–A–Cake

Traditional Mother Goose

Pat-a-cake, pat-a-cake, baker's man,
Bake me a cake as fast as you can.
Pat it and prick it and mark it with a "T,"
And put it in the oven for Tommy and me.

Cake

Using a cake mix from the store, bake it as the directions indicate. Frost the cake using any of the commercially available frostings. After frosting, mark the cake with a T, using red hot candies or M&Ms.

ಇ൴ ಇ൴ ಇ൴

Teddy Bear Baker

Phoebe and Selby Worthington
Puffin Books, 1979

The teddy bear baker bakes cakes, pies, and breads and delivers them to his friends in town. He enjoys tea and muffins with raspberry jam before going to bed after his full day. The recipe below is for an easy cake, but your children might want to have tea and muffins, or bake a pie or a loaf of bread with the recipes listed elsewhere in this book.

Teddy Bear's Cake

In a 9x13" pan, layer:

1 can crushed pineapple in heavy syrup
1 can cherry pie filling
2 sticks of margarine, cut up and dotted over all
1 yellow cake mix, sprinkled over top

Bake at 350° for 55 minutes.

There's a Hippopotamus on Our Roof Eating Cake

Hazel Edwards
Illustrated by Deborah Niland
Holiday House, 1980

There's a hippopotamus on the roof riding his bike, taking a shower, and drawing with crayons as well as eating cake. The little girl in this book imagines that there's a hippo doing all the things she wishes she could do.

Special Cake

2 cups sugar

2 sticks margarine

4 eggs

2 teaspoons vanilla

1 cup milk

1 box graham crackers, crumbled

2 cups nuts

1 cup crushed pineapple, drained

Combine sugar and margarine; mix in eggs. Add vanilla, milk, and cracker crumbs. Fold in nuts and pineapple. Place in 9x13" greased pan and bake in preheated 350° oven for 45 minutes or until done.

Benny Bakes a Cake

Eve Rice
Greenwillow, 1981

It is Benny's birthday. He and Ralph the dog help Mom bake a birthday cake. While the cake cools, Ralph can wait no longer and he eats the cake. Benny is disappointed, but Dad saves the birthday celebration with another cake.

This cake is so good that your children and the neighborhood dogs might want to eat it before it is cool, too!

Chocolate Birthday Cake

1 pkg. chocolate instant pudding

1 pkg. chocolate cake mix

4 eggs

1 cup water

¼ cup cooking oil

Combine the ingredients in a bowl and beat with electric mixer at medium speed for 2 minutes. Grease and flour a bundt pan. Bake in a 350° oven for about an hour, or until a toothpick comes out clean. Cool for 15 minutes and then remove from pan. Continue to cool cake on a rack. Sprinkle with powdered sugar.

Happy Birthday!

Gail Gibbons
Holiday House, 1986

Gail Gibbons explains many of our birthday traditions in a simple and colorful manner. Of course with this book you will want to bake and decorate a birthday cake!

Lemon Birthday Cake

1 pkg. lemon cake mix

1 pkg. lemon instant pudding

4 eggs, unbeaten

¾ cup cooking oil

¾ cup water

Place all ingredients in bowl and beat until well-blended. Grease a 9x13" cake pan. Bake for 40 minutes at 350°.

Remove the cake from the oven and pierce the entire surface with a fork. While the cake is still hot, pour the following topping over all:

Topping

Mix together:

2 cups sifted powdered sugar

⅓ cup orange juice

2 tablespoons cooking oil

Little Bear Learns to Read the Cookbook

Janice
Illustrated by Mariana
Lothrop, Lee, Shepard, 1969

Little Bear feels as though he cannot do anything. He cannot make milk like the cow, or give eggs like the chicken. He goes to school and learns to read the cookbook. Now he can make the finest chocolate cake!

Chocolate Cake

1½ cups sugar

1⅓ cups flour

2 teaspoons baking powder

3 tablespoons cocoa

1½ teaspoons baking soda

1 teaspoon salt

½ cup oil

1¼ cups milk

2 eggs

2 teaspoons vanilla

Mix together the sugar, flour, baking powder, cocoa, baking soda, and salt. Add the oil, milk, eggs, and vanilla. Pour into a greased cake pan. Bake for 45 minutes at 350°. Frost if desired.

The Duchess Bakes a Cake

Virginia Kahn
Charles Scribner's Sons, 1955

When the Duchess becomes bored of her embroidery and tired of talking, she decides to bake a lovely light luscious delectable cake for her family.

Light and Lovely Cake

2 cans pie filling, any flavor
1 box of yellow cake mix
1 stick melted butter
sprinkle of cinnamon
chopped nuts, optional

Grease an 8x8" cake pan. Put in pie filling. Sprinkle dry cake mix over pie filling. Pour the melted butter on the top. Sprinkle a little cinnamon over all. Add chopped nuts to top if desired. Bake for 40 minutes in a 375° oven.

❧   ❧   ❧

Oh, Lewis!

Eve Rice
Macmillan, 1974

Your students will relate to Lewis as he struggles to keep his winter outerwear zipped, tied, and all in place. After a cold romp in the snow, enjoy hot tea and chocolate cake, as Lewis does.

Hot Tea

Make a pot of regular tea, or mix up a batch of spiced tea to sip on a cold winter's day.

⅓ cup sugar

1 pkg. lemonade mix

*1 cup instant orange
 breakfast drink*

½ teaspoon allspice

⅓ cup instant tea

1 teaspoon cinnamon

Mix the dry ingredients well. When you are ready to have a cup of tea, add 2 teaspoons of mixture to 1 cup of boiling water.

Chocolate Cake

This is an easy cake to make because you mix all the ingredients right in the cake pan.

1½ cups flour

1 cup sugar

1 teaspoon baking soda

1 teaspoon baking powder

1 teaspoon salt

*3 tablespoons unsweetened
 cocoa powder*

5 tablespoons oil

1 teaspoon vinegar

1 teaspoon vanilla

1 cup water

powdered sugar

Combine dry ingredients in an ungreased 8" square pan. Make three holes in the mixture. Pour oil in one hole, vinegar in one hole, and vanilla in one hole. Pour water over all and mix with a fork until blended. Bake 35 to 40 minutes at 350°. Cool and sprinkle with powdered sugar.

The Tale of Peter Rabbit

Beatrix Potter
Frederick Warne and Co., 1902

This well-known and well-loved book about Flopsy, Mopsy, Cottontail, and Peter is familiar to many children. If your students are not familiar with Peter Rabbit, be sure to share this delightful book with them while they eat bread, milk, and blackberries like the three good little rabbits—Flopsy, Mopsy, and Cottontail.

Bread, Milk, and Blackberries

Bake some bread (see recipe listed with *The Little Red Hen* or *The Giant Jam Sandwich*) or enjoy a good crusty bakery bread. Let the children wash some blackberries, put them in a bowl, and eat them covered with milk.

Camomile Tea

Peter, too ill to enjoy bread, berries, and milk, is given some camomile tea. You might wish to make a pot and serve it to the class. If this tea is not available at your supermarket, try a health food store.

Ernest and Celestine's Picnic

Gabrielle Vincent
Greenwillow, 1982

Ernest and Celestine plan to go on the best picnic ever. But when they wake up in the morning, it is raining. Celestine is very disappointed. They decide to take their picnic of sandwiches and tea, build a rain shelter, and pretend the sun is shining.

Sandwiches and Tea

Have each student make a honey or Swiss cheese sandwich just like Ernest and Celestine do. And don't forget the pot of tea. This would be a great book and activity to share on a rainy day or if a picnic you plan gets rained out. Have a picnic in the rain just like Ernest and Celestine!

Poll Parrot

Traditional Mother Goose

Little Poll Parrot
Sat in his garret,
Eating toast and tea;
A little brown mouse
Jumped into the house
And stole it all away.

Toast and Tea

Bring a toaster to school and let each child make a piece of toast. Have on hand some butter and various jams and jellies that they can spread on their toast.

Bring 1 tea bag per child and give each one some water just at the boiling point. Steep the tea for about 1 minute. Have sugar and cream available for those who may want it.

૪ ૪ ૪

May I Bring a Friend?

Caldecott Award Book

*Beatrice Schenk de Regniers
Illustrated by Ben Montresor
Atheneum, 1964*

Each time the king and queen invite a little boy to tea, breakfast, or dinner, he wants to bring a friend. The king and queen always agree for "any friend of our friend is welcome here." But they are always surprised at the unusual types and the number of friends that he has. When you have tea with your class, they might want to invite a stuffed animal friend to join them.

Tea

Have a variety of herbal teas available for your students to choose from. Give them the choice of adding honey, lemon, or milk to their tea. Make the tea party special by using a cloth tablecloth and napkins.

ﻉﻠ ﻉﻠ ﻉﻠ

Polly Put the Kettle On

Traditional Mother Goose

Polly put the kettle on,
Polly put the kettle on,
Polly put the kettle on,
We'll all have tea.

Sukey took it off again,
Sukey took it off again,
Sukey took it off again,
They're all gone away.

Tea

1 tea bag per child
1 cup water per child

Boil the water in a teakettle until it whistles. Pour water into a cup with a tea bag and let the tea steep for about 1 minute. Provide sugar and cream for those who desire it.

Alice in Wonderland

Lewis Carroll
Scholastic Books, originally published 1865

Invite your students to a Mad Tea Party based on the one in *Alice in Wonderland*. Use several teapots and fancy teacups rather than disposable cups for this special celebration. Your children might enjoy wearing silly clothes, or wearing their clothes inside out and backwards to add to the madness of the tea party. They might each want to tell a riddle or joke at the party. Wouldn't this be a fun party to invite the mothers and/or fathers to?

ٿ ٿ ٿ

Good Lemonade

Illustrated by Marie Zimmerman
Franklin Watts, 1976

If you are going to have a lemonade stand and you want to have more customers than just your brother, you are going to have to serve *good lemonade*.

Fresh-Squeezed Lemonade

For each child you will need:

½ lemon

1½–2 cups water

2–3 tablespoons sugar

Roll lemons on table before cutting; this makes a juicier lemon. Cut lemon in half and squeeze using a manual or electric juicer. Add water. Stir in sugar to taste. Use lots of ice cubes and enjoy the taste of fresh lemonade!

Happy Winter

Karen Gunderheimer
Harper and Row, 1982

A little girl, her sister, and their mother celebrate on a cold winter day. They enjoy many activities and several kinds of food including pancakes, orange juice, and tea for breakfast. They also bake a fudge cake and drink hot cocoa. The recipe for the fudge cake is included in this book. The recipe below is for the hot cocoa to drink with the Happy Winter Fudge Cake.

Hot Cocoa

8 cups powdered milk

1½ cups sugar

1 lb. chocolate drink mix

8 oz. dry non-dairy creamer

Mix all ingredients together. Store in a gallon-sized airtight container. When you are ready to serve the cocoa, you will need 1 cup boiling water and ¼ cup hot cocoa mix for each child.

George and Martha

James Marshall
Houghton Mifflin, 1972

George and Martha are hippos and are very good friends. Martha loves to make split pea soup. She makes pot after pot of soup for George. George, however, hates split pea soup but he doesn't know how to tell Martha. When she catches him pouring the soup into his shoes, he finally admits to her that he hates split pea soup. They agree that honesty is the best way to keep a friend and Martha admits she hates to eat the soup, too, she only likes to make it. They decide Martha will make chocolate chip cookies instead.

Split Pea Soup

1 pkg. split green peas

1 onion, diced

1 potato, diced

3 carrots, diced

a ham bone, ham hocks, or fresh Canadian bacon

salt and pepper to taste

Soak the peas overnight. Drain off excess water. Add 1½ gallons of fresh water, onion, potato, carrots, and ham. Bring to a boil and simmer 1½ to 2 hours.

Watch Out for Chicken Feet in Your Soup

Tomie dePaola
Prentice Hall, 1974

Joey and his friend visit Joey's grandmother. Grandmother feeds the boys well and makes them each a bread doll. The bread doll recipe is included in the book. You might also wish to make spaghetti (see the recipe on page 23) or chicken soup. Oh, and watch out for the chicken feet!

Chicken Soup

1 whole chicken, or 1 pkg. of chicken parts

2 onions, quartered

2–3 carrots, sliced

3–4 chicken flavor bouillon cubes

1–2 celery sticks, diced

1 bay leaf

Put all the ingredients in a pot. Cover with water. Heat to a boil and then simmer about 1½ hours or until chicken falls off the bone easily. Bone the chicken and throw away the bones.

Growing Vegetable Soup

Lois Ehlert
Harcourt Brace Jovanovich, 1987

This is a colorful book about planting and growing a vegetable garden. The pictures are bright and vivid. You can make the vegetable soup using the recipe included in the book or use the following soup recipe:

Vegetable Soup

1 onion, diced

1½ cups celery, sliced

2 potatoes, diced

3 fresh tomatoes, or 1 large can tomatoes

1½ teaspoons salt

1½ cups carrots, sliced

1 cup shredded cabbage

Put ingredients in a pot and cook until the vegetables are tender. Add barley to thicken if desired.

Kevin's Grandma

Barbara Williams
Illustrated by Kay Choaro
E. P. Dutton, 1975

Kevin's grandma is like no other. She scuba-dives, jumps from airplanes, climbs mountains, and makes homemade peanut butter soup! "Whoever heard of peanut butter soup?"

Actually, peanut butter soup is very popular in Africa. Maybe when your students make this soup they will believe everything about Kevin's grandma.

Peanut Butter Soup

4 cans (14½ oz.) chicken broth

16 oz. jar peanut butter

1 medium onion, chopped

1 tablespoon cornstarch

1½ cups half-and-half

salt and pepper

sprig of fresh parsley

Heat the chicken broth, peanut butter, and onion. Bring to a boil, stirring occasionally. Mix cornstarch with the half-and-half. Add this mixture to the soup. Add salt and pepper to taste. Simmer for 30 minutes. Garnish with fresh parsley.

Chicken Soup with Rice

Maurice Sendak
Harper and Row, 1962

Make it once, make it twice, make some chicken soup with rice! This book is written in rhyme and it includes a rhyme for each month of the year. Try to find a copy of the small version of this book in The Nutshell Library. You can heat several cans of chicken soup with rice or make the following recipe:

Chicken Soup with Rice

8 cups seasoned chicken broth

1 cup chopped celery

½ cup rice

Heat broth; add celery and cook until celery is tender. Add rice and cook until it is fluffy.

If you want to add more vegetables, such as carrots, onions, or spices such as bay leaves, add them when you put in the celery.

Stone Soup

Caldecott Honor Book

Marcia Brown
Charles Scribner's Sons, 1947

Three hungry soldiers convince the villagers to share their food by showing them how to make soup from a stone. This is a good meal for the children to make and share—with the book—with another class.

Have each child bring a vegetable to contribute to the making of stone soup. Several children can bring the same vegetables so everyone can bring an ingredient.

Stone Soup

3 smooth, clean stones *zucchini*
canned or fresh corn *green beans*
canned or fresh peas *1½ lbs. hamburger*
potatoes *garlic*
carrots *onions*
celery *beef bouillon cubes*
fresh or canned tomatoes

Have each child wash and chop the vegetable that he or she brought and put it into the soup pot. Brown the hamburger, garlic, and onions; put in with the vegetables. Add water to cover. Dissolve 3 or 4 bouillon cubes and add to the soup mixture. Cook on medium heat until the potatoes and carrots are tender. Serve with crackers.

Nail Soup

Retold by Harve Zemach
Illustrated by Margot Zemach
Follett, 1964

Nail Soup is another version of the story *Stone Soup*. This time a nail is used to make the soup instead of a stone.

Nail Soup

Use the recipe listed with the book *Stone Soup* on page 73. Or open several cans of chunky-style vegetable soup and add a nail for "extra flavoring." Be sure to wash the nail before adding it to the soup, as some new nails have a light coating of oil to prevent rust.

ஃ ஃ ஃ

"Birthday Soup" from Little Bear

Else Holmelund
Illustrated by Maurice Sendak
Harper and Row, 1957

When Little Bear thinks his mother has forgotten to bake a cake for his birthday, he makes birthday soup for his friends who come to celebrate with him. While they are eating soup, Mother arrives with a surprise—a big birthday cake. She didn't forget his birthday after all!

Birthday Soup

Instead of assigning a specific vegetable to each child in class, ask them to just bring in any vegetable to put into the soup. You might want to buy cans of beef or chicken broth and some meat to add to the soup. Let the children wash and cut up the vegetables that they have chosen to add to the soup. Add enough water to cover the vegetables and cook until they are tender. What a wonderful birthday surprise soup!

❧ ❧ ❧

My Kitchen

Harlow Rockwell
Greenwillow, 1980

A child takes the reader on a tour through his kitchen and explains how he makes his lunch of chicken noodle soup, a peanut butter sandwich, and milk.

Soup and Sandwich

2 large cans of chicken noodle soup
bread
peanut butter
milk

Prepare the soup according to the directions on the can. Each child makes his or her own peanut butter sandwich and pours a glass of milk.

The Gingerbread Man

Retold and illustrated by Paul Galdone
Houghton Mifflin, Co., 1975

In this familiar tale, the gingerbread man gets chased through the countryside by the little old woman, the little old man, and many others. This recipe for gingerbread men is great because you do not have to roll out the dough. Give each child a little ball and have them mold it as they would clay. You do have to watch them carefully, as the children do not mold the cookies with a consistent thickness. Some may tend to burn while others are not quite ready. Keep checking the cookies, using the time given very generally.

Gingerbread Men

1 cup brown sugar	*1 teaspoon ground ginger*
¾ cup shortening	*½ teaspoon allspice*
1 egg	*1 teaspoon baking soda*
¼ cup molasses	*2 teaspoons cinnamon*
2 cups flour	*raisins for eyes*

Combine sugar and shortening. Mix in egg and molasses. Combine dry ingredients in separate bowl, then combine with dough mixture. Refrigerate for 20 minutes.

Give each child a piece of aluminum foil and let them mold the cookie dough as they would modeling clay. Provide raisins or red hot candies for eyes, mouth, and buttons, if you desire. Bake at 350° for about 10 minutes; allow more time for the thicker cookie pieces and less time for the thin ones. Let cookies cool slightly before removing them from the pan. They may be decorated with icing after cooling if you desire. Doesn't your kitchen smell good?

The Doorbell Rang

Pat Hutchins
Greenwillow, 1986

There are twelve cookies for Victoria and Sam to share, until the doorbell rings. Each time the doorbell rings, more visitors come and the cookies must be divided up among all the company. All goes well until twelve friends are gathered at the table and the doorbell rings. What will they do? They have no more cookies to divide!

When you make these chocolate chip cookies, be sure to make a few extra in case someone shows up at *your* door.

Chocolate Chip Cookies

¼ cup brown sugar

½ cup sugar

½ cup shortening

1 egg, beaten

2 teaspoons vanilla

1 cup flour

¾ teaspoon baking soda

½ teaspoon salt

3 oz. chopped nuts

1 cup chocolate chips

Cream the sugars with the shortening. Stir in egg and vanilla. Combine dry ingredients; add to sugar-shortening mixture. Add nuts and chocolate chips. Bake on a lightly greased cookie sheet for 8 to 10 minutes in preheated 350° oven. Makes about 3 dozen.

If You Give a Mouse a Cookie

Laura Joffe Numeroff
Illustrated by Felicia Bond
Harper and Row, 1985

If you give a mouse a cookie he is going to want a glass of milk. What will happen if you give him the milk? You will have to decide whether you will share these cookies with a mouse or not!

Chocolate Chip Cookies

1 cup brown sugar

½ cup margarine

2 tablespoons water

1 egg, beaten

2 teaspoons vanilla

½ teaspoon baking soda

1 cup flour

½ teaspoon salt

6 oz. pkg. chocolate chips

Thoroughly combine sugar and margarine, then add water, egg, and vanilla. Combine with baking soda, flour, and salt. Stir in chocolate chips. Drop dough onto a greased cookie sheet. Bake at 375° for about 10 minutes. Makes about 2 dozen cookies.

"Cookies"
from Frog and Toad Together

Newbery Honor Book
Reading Rainbow Selection

Arnold Lobel
Harper and Row, 1972

In the story "Cookies," Toad makes some cookies and takes them over to his friend Frog's house. The cookies are delicious and Frog and Toad have a difficult time controlling the urge to eat them all.

No-Bake Chocolate Chip Cookies

4 tablespoons cocoa

2 cups sugar

½ cup margarine

½ cup milk

½ cup chopped nuts

½ cup peanut butter

2 teaspoons vanilla

3 cups oatmeal

Combine cocoa, sugar, margarine, and milk in pot. Boil for 3 minutes. Remove from heat and add nuts, peanut butter, vanilla, and oats. Beat until well blended. Drop small amounts of mixture onto aluminum foil.

Chocolate Chip Cookie Contest

Barbara Douglass
Lothrop, Lee and Shepard, 1985

Kevin plans to enter the chocolate chip cookie contest at the mall but he needs to find an adult to help him use the oven. Every adult he asks is too busy to help, but each gives some advice as to what ingredient is missing from his recipe. When he finally finds a grown-up to help him, they make a chocolate chip pizza. Do they win the contest? You be the judge when you make the chocolate chip pizza using the recipe included in the book.

Chocolate Chip Pizza

Have each child bring six of his or her favorite chocolate chip cookies to school. Make the chocolate chip pizza using the recipe in the book and have your own Chocolate Chip Contest. Taste all the different types of cookies. Have a blue ribbon for each child to award the cookie he or she liked the best. Every child will have a ribbon to take home to remember the day's activities.

🌰 🌰 🌰

Arthur's Christmas Cookies

Lillian Hoban
Harper and Row, 1972

When Arthur tries to make his mother and father some Christmas cookies, they turn out as hard as a rock and very salty. Arthur is disappointed until he realizes he can paint his salt cookies and hang them on the Christmas tree. Your students can make salt dough ornaments for holiday giving. They aren't edible, but they are pretty—and fun!

Salt Dough "Cookies"

4 cups flour

1 cup salt

1½ cups water

Mix flour and salt together. Slowly add water until dough is firm but pliable. You might not need to use the full cup and a half of water. Knead dough on a floured cutting board for 8 to 10 minutes, until smooth.

This dough can be shaped by hand like clay, or rolled and cut with cookie cutters. To make cookies like Arthur's, use star, angel, reindeer, and bell-shaped cookie cutters. Poke a hole at the top large enough to thread a ribbon through. Bake at 350° for an hour or more, depending on the thickness of the dough.

This dough can be painted or left natural. (Do anything you want with it except eat it!) Store finished ornaments in a dry area. Store unbaked dough in an airtight container in the refrigerator.

Hot Chocolate

While you make your dough ornaments, enjoy a cup of hot chocolate, as Arthur did. For each child you will need:

1 cup milk

1 tablespoon pre-sweetened chocolate milk mix

1 marshmallow

1 candy cane (optional)

Let the children mix the chocolate milk mix with their milk. Pour all cups of milk into pot and heat until it is warm. Place a marshmallow in the bottom of the cup before pouring in the hot chocolate. Stir with a candy cane.

"Eighteen Flavors"
from Where the Sidewalk Ends

Shel Silverstein
Harper and Row, 1974

In this popular book of poetry you will find a poem about an ice cream cone with 18 flavors. You can buy most of the flavors at the grocery store or ice cream shop, but you might want to try making your own. Here are two different recipes for homemade ice cream. You need an ice cream maker for one, and just a freezer for the other.

Pumpkin Ice Cream

1½ cups sugar
1 large egg
2 cups whipping cream
1 cup pumpkin
2 cups half-and-half
⅛ teaspoon allspice
2 teaspoons cinnamon
¼ teaspoon nutmeg
1 teaspoon vanilla
rock salt
10 lb. bag of ice

Beat sugar and egg together. Add remaining ingredients, except rock salt and ice. Pour into freezer part of the ice cream maker. Alternate ice and rock salt in container that surrounds the freezer. Let the children take turns cranking the ice cream maker until ice cream freezes. Replace ice and rock salt as the ice melts.

Lemon Ice Cream

2 cups whipping cream
1 cup sugar
⅓ cup lemon juice, freshly squeezed
1 tablespoon grated lemon peel

Stir together cream and sugar. Add lemon juice and lemon peel. Pour into a small cake pan. Freeze about 4½ hours, or until firm.

Hansel and Gretel

Caldecott Honor Book

Retold by Rika Lesser
Illustrated by Paul Zelinsky
Dodd, Mead, and Co., 1984

This Caldecott Honor Book is illustrated with great detail. Your students will enjoy making a miniature candy house.

Candy House

Frosting Cement:

2 egg whites

½ teaspoon cream of tartar

2 cups powdered sugar

6 graham crackers per child

1 empty half-pint milk carton per child

Beat the egg whites and the cream of tartar until stiff. Add the powdered sugar and beat 5 more minutes with an electric mixer. This frosting can be used to cement your candy house together, and it will harden when it dries. Using graham crackers and the frosting, let your students cement the crackers to the half-pint milk carton for the base of the house. Cement candies on the cube with the cement frosting to look like a candy house. These work well: small hard candies, such as red hots, M&Ms, Reese's Pieces, Life Savers, colorful cereals, peppermint candies, gumdrops, cookie sprinkles, chocolate chips, or mini marshmallows.

The Hungry Thing

Jan Sleplan and Ann Seidler
Illustrated by Richard E. Martin
Scholastic Book Services, 1967

When the hungry thing asks for feetloaf, and a fanana, your children will quickly figure out what he is hungry for. You might want to buy a bag of gollipops—I mean lollipops—or you may want to make your own.

"Gollipops"

36 lollipop sticks

½ cup butter

1½ cups sugar

1 cup light corn syrup

food coloring

peppermint flavoring

Grease a cookie sheet or line it with waxed paper. Arrange sticks on cookie sheet, leaving lots of space between them. Combine butter, sugar, and corn syrup in a pan. Heat mixture until it starts to boil. Cook on medium heat, stirring occasionally, until it reaches 270° on a candy thermometer. Be sure to use extreme caution around this hot liquid. Remove from heat. Add food coloring and flavoring. Quickly spoon candy over sticks, keeping candy as round as you can. Remove from cookie sheet when cooled completely.

The Lion, the Witch and the Wardrobe

C. S. Lewis
Macmillan, 1953

This is the first of seven books written about the magical land of Narnia. Lucy, Susan, and Peter must rescue their brother, Eustace, from the alluring and wicked White Witch, who tempts him with the sweetness of Turkish Delight.

Turkish Delight

2 tablespoons water

⅔ cup fruit pectin

½ teaspoon baking soda

1 cup corn syrup, light

¾ cup sugar

¼ cup raspberry jelly

2 tablespoons frozen orange juice concentrate, thawed

1 tablespoon lemon juice

½ cup chopped nuts

In a large pot, stir water and pectin together. Add baking soda (the mixture will foam). In a second pan, combine corn syrup and sugar. Heat the ingredients in both pans. Heat the pectin until the foam has stopped and heat the sugar solution until it boils. As the sugar boils, pour in the pectin. Stir in jelly and orange juice for 1 minute. Remove from heat and add lemon juice and nuts. Pour into an 8" square pan. Let stand for several hours at room temperature until firm. Sprinkle with powdered sugar.

Yummers!

James Marshall
Houghton Mifflin, 1973

Emily Pig is on a diet and invites her friend Eugene to go for a walk with her. All this exercise makes Emily hungry. As she walks, she finds excuses to eat—and eat she does!

After enjoying this book you might want to serve something as easy as a small dish of peach ice cream, or you may want to set up a do-it-yourself banana split bar.

Banana Split Bar

Each child can bring in an ingredient. Put them into small bowls. Allow each child to create his or her own banana split. You might wish to include:

bananas, peeled and sliced lengthwise

2 gallons of ice cream

chocolate syrup

candy sprinkles

butterscotch sauce

chopped nuts

maraschino cherries

shredded coconut

whipped cream

Handy Pandy

Traditional Mother Goose

Handy Pandy, Jack-a-dandy,
Loves plum cake and sugar candy.
He bought some at the grocer's shop
And out he came, hop, hop, hop.

Sugar Candy

2 cups sugar

½ teaspoon cinnamon

4½ cups nuts (pecans, walnuts)

1 cup water

Combine all ingredients in an electric skillet. Heat until liquid evaporates. Place nuts on a baking sheet and divide into bite-sized pieces. Cool.

❧ ❧ ❧

"Stout's Candy" from The Giant's Farm

Jane Yolen
Illustrated by Tomie dePaola
The Seabury Press, 1977

This book contains five short stories about five giants who lived together on a farm. In the story "Stout's Candy," Stout, the fattest of the giants, wants to make candy but discovers that though he has all the ingredients needed, he doesn't have any tsp. or tbsp. or a c. as called for in the recipe. Dab, the smallest giant, explains that tsp. means teaspoon, tbsp. is tablespoon, and c. stands for cup. Stout is now happy, as he can make his no-bake candy.

The recipe for Stout's Giant No-Cook Bon Bons is included in *The Giant's Farm*. The children will be as happy as Stout when they try this candy.

ã. ã. ã.

Jelly Beans for Breakfast

Mariam Young
Illustrated by Beverly Komoda
Parents' Magazine Press, 1968

Come to my house and we'll have all the fun in the world! We'll ride our bikes to the moon, we'll play gypsies, have beds made of twigs covered with moss, and we'll have jelly beans for breakfast!

Jelly Beans

A bag or two of jelly beans will delight your students when you pretend that you are eating them for breakfast. Serve with orange juice to create a breakfast atmosphere.

Chocolate Fever

Robert Kinmmel Smith
Dell, 1972

❧   ❧   ❧

Charlie and the Chocolate Factory

Roald Dahl
Bantam Skylark, 1964

❧   ❧   ❧

The Chocolate Touch

Patrick Skene Catling
Bantam, Skylark, 1952

After reading these books, buy each child a chocolate bar or small chocolate candies. If you prefer, you might even want to make chocolate candies. You will need candy molds and chocolate pieces, both available at candy stores or hobby and craft stores.

Fish for Supper

Caldecott Honor Book

M. B. Goffstein
E. P. Dutton, 1976

Grandmother loves to get up at five o'clock in the morning and go fishing all day. She comes home in the evening and fries her catch for supper. She cleans up fast, so she can go to bed and get up and go fishing again.

If you can take your class fishing, you can prepare your catch at school the next day. If not, buy some fresh or frozen fish at the store.

Fried Fish

1 egg yolk
½ cup ice water
¾ cup self-rising flour
1–2 lbs. cod fillets or other fish, at least ½" thick

In a mixing bowl, beat the egg yolk; add ice water and beat again until well blended. Add flour and stir in but do not stir until smooth; mixture should be lumpy. The batter must be kept cold. You might want to make the batter and store in the refrigerator for a couple of hours before cooking. Heat up some cooking oil in an electric skillet. When the oil is hot, dip the fish into the batter and fry until crispy and golden brown.

Fishy, Fishy in the Brook

Traditional Mother Goose

Fishy, fishy in the brook,
Daddy caught him on a hook,
Mommy fried him in a pan,
Baby eats him like a man.

Fish Sticks

1 or 2 fish sticks per child

Fry up the fish sticks in a small amount of oil in an electric skillet. If you want to fry fresh or frozen fish, see the recipe listed under *Fish for Supper* on page 91.

❧ ❧ ❧

Merry Christmas, Strega Nona

Tomie dePaola
Harcourt Brace Jovanovich, 1986

Here's another adventure with Big Anthony and Strega Nona. This time Strega Nona almost doesn't have her annual Christmas celebration because of Big Anthony's laziness. He forgets to soak the codfish—the *baccala*—for the codfish stew. What will Strega Nona do?

Codfish Stew

Baccala, or dried salt cod, needs to be soaked for several days before using. If you cannot find dried salt cod, substitute fresh or frozen cod. But if the children can see how long it takes to prepare the salt cod before it can be cooked, they will better understand why Strega Nona was so disappointed with Big Anthony.

Wash the salted cod under cold running water, then totally immerse it in cold water, cover, and keep in the refrigerator 24 to 48 hours. Change the water two or three times during this soaking period.

When ready to cook, place the cod in boiling water and simmer 15 minutes. Drain. When cool, remove bones and skin.

½ lb. codfish cut in bite-sized pieces

2–3 potatoes

1–2 stalks of celery

1–2 onions

2–3 garlic cloves

½ teaspoon thyme

1½ teaspoons dried parsley

corn, peas, green pepper, mushrooms, or other vegetables

Chop the vegetables and simmer all ingredients about 15 minutes.

The Great Brain

John D. Fitzgerald
Dell Publishing Co., 1975

Tom Fitzgerald, better known as The Great Brain, is always scheming of ways to get out of household chores and ways to make money. Tom loves all kinds of fish because fish is known as brain food. You might enjoy tasting codfish, as Tom does in this book.

Codfish

2–4 lbs. cod fillets

salt and pepper

corn meal

butter

lemon

Sprinkle the salt, pepper, and corn meal on fish. Melt 2 tablespoons of butter in a pan. Brown fish in butter; turn and brown other side. Serve with melted butter and lemon wedges.

The Island

Gary Paulsen
Orchard Books, 1988

When Wil Neuton and his family move from Madison, Wisconsin, to the northern woods of Wisconsin, he is very disappointed. He cannot understand what the northern woods have to offer until he discovers the island. Wil decides to camp on the island and makes discoveries—not only about the island, but also some very important ones about himself and his family.

Camp Food

Wil lived on canned food while camping on the island. Perhaps you could set up camp in your classroom, schoolyard, or backyard at home.

canned stew

canned beans

fruit cocktail

Just open the cans and eat—no need to heat them if you are going to experience mealtime as Wil does!

My Side of the Mountain

Newbery Honor Book

Jean George
E. P. Dutton, 1959

Sam Gribley sets out to live completely self-sufficiently in a remote area in the Catskill Mountains. He builds a shelter in a tree and lives off the land for all his needs.

Sam eats various types of food that he gathers or hunts in the woods, including deer, mussels, rabbit, acorns, tubers of wild flowers, and sassafras root. Your children might want to enjoy rabbit stew while reading this book.

Rabbit Stew

2½ lbs. rabbit, pieced	*2 teaspoons salt*
1¼ cups water	*½ teaspoon pepper*
¾ cup vinegar	*⅓ cup flour*
1 onion	*⅓ cup shortening*
2 bay leaves	*2 tablespoons brown sugar*
8 whole cloves	*1 cup sour cream*

Put rabbit in a glass bowl and cover with water and vinegar. Add onion and spices, but reserve 1 teaspoon salt, and cover. Marinate in refrigerator for three days. Remove the meat from marinade but do not discard marinade; coat meat with flour and remaining salt. Fry in hot shortening, turning frequently, until brown. Strain one cup vinegar and water mixture to remove pieces of spices. Add brown sugar to strained marinade and pour over meat. Cover and simmer until tender. Add sour cream just before serving; do not boil.

The Magic Meatballs

Alan Yaffe
Illustrated by Karen Born Andersen
Dial Press, 1979

Poor Marvin—everyone in the family bosses him around, until one day when a strange man gives him some magic meat! After Marvin eats the meatballs made from this meat, unusual things begin to happen at home.

Magic Meatballs

Be careful who you share your magic meatballs with!

1 egg, slightly beaten

½ cup milk

2 slices bread, diced

1 lb. hamburger

¼ teaspoon pepper

1 onion, finely chopped

½ teaspoon salt

2–3 teaspoons butter

Combine all the ingredients except the butter. Each child makes a 1″ meatball. Brown the meatballs in the butter using an electric skillet.

On Top of Spaghetti

Tom Glazer
Illustrated by Tom Garcia
Doubleday and Co., Inc., 1963

This book is an illustrated version of the popular silly song "On Top of Spaghetti." Included with the pictures are the music and words to the song. You might even want to plant a meatball to see if you can grow a meatball tree.

Meatballs

1 lb. hamburger

½ cup bread crumbs

1 egg

1 teaspoon salt

¼ teaspoon pepper

Mix all the ingredients in a bowl. Let each child make a small meatball. Brown in an electric skillet, turning the meatballs as they cook.

Cloudy with a Chance of Meatballs

Judi Barrett
Illustrated by Ron Barrett
Atheneum, 1978

There are no grocery stores in the town of Chewandswallow. Instead, it rains there three times a day—at breakfast, lunch, and dinner. If you would prefer to make a spaghetti-type meatball, see the recipe listed with the book *On Top of Spaghetti* on page 98.

Meatballs

1 lb. hamburger

½ lb. veal

¼ lb. pork

¾ cup bread crumbs

1 egg

½ cup chopped onions

1 cup milk

1½ teaspoons salt

½ teaspoon pepper

½ teaspoon nutmeg

dash of allspice and parsley

Mix all ingredients. Let the children shape a meatball or two. Brown meatballs in a skillet. Serve as is, or mix up a package of dry sour cream mix, using about ¼ cup more milk than the directions call for. Coat the meatballs with the sour cream mixture.

Meat Pies and Sausage

Dorothy O. Van Woerhom
Illustrated by Joseph Low
Greenwillow, 1976

In the first of three short stories in this book, a wolf angers a fox by eating his breakfast. When the wolf further torments the fox by threatening to eat him, the fox outwits the wolf. The fox takes the wolf to the house of Ivan and Nessa with the promise of eating meat pies. They sneak into the cellar. What becomes of the fox and the wolf?

Meat Pies

1–1½ lbs. hamburger

2 onions, diced

1⅓ cups mushrooms

1½ teaspoons salt

1½ teaspoons pepper

1 tube crescent rolls

1–1½ cups sour cream

2 eggs

Brown hamburger, onions, mushrooms, salt, and pepper. Line a casserole dish with crescent rolls. Pour in hamburger mixture. Blend the sour cream and eggs. Spread over hamburger. Bake at 350° for 35 minutes.

Don't Forget the Bacon

Pat Hutchins
Greenwillow, 1976

In order to remember the grocery list, a little boy makes a game of the things his mother asks him to buy. He is reminded, "Don't forget the bacon." Guess what he forgets! After reading this book, your children will enjoy frying their own strips of bacon.

Bacon

Using an electric skillet, have an adult fry up a piece of bacon for each child. Be sure to have plenty of supervision around the hot bacon grease.

The Day It Rained Watermelons

Mabel Watts
Illustrated by Lee Anderson
E. M. Hale, 1967

Farmer O'Dell gets up on the wrong side of the bed one day and is late getting to the market square, where he has to take a truck full of watermelons. As he travels the bumpy roads, the watermelons tumble out the back of his truck. He doesn't discover this until he gets to the market square and finds only three watermelons in the back of his truck. What will he do now?

Watermelon

Buy a watermelon and, taking care not to lose it out the back of your car, bring it to school. Let the children help you slice it up for a refreshing snack. You might want to buy a yellow watermelon for the children to try.

Cherries and Cherry Pits

Vera B. Williams
Greenwillow, 1986

Bidemmi is a little girl who loves to write and illustrate with markers. Every story she writes has something in common—they are all about sharing and eating cherries. Share a bowl of cherries with your students and let them write and illustrate as they eat. Maybe they would also like to plant the cherry pits.

Cherries

Buy two or three pints of cherries and let the children wash them and remove the stems. When they eat them, remind them to watch out for the cherry pits.

Cantaloupes

Traditional Mother Goose

Cantaloupes! Cantaloupes!
What is the price?
Eight for a dollar,
And all very nice.

Cantaloupes

Bring a cantaloupe or two to school. Help the children cut the melons into either wedges or small pieces.

Mr. Rabbit and the Lovely Present

Caldecott Honor Book

Charlotte Zolotow
Illustrated by Maurice Sendak
Harper and Row, 1962

When a little girl cannot decide what to give her mother for her birthday, she receives the help of a rabbit. After much discussion, a perfect present is found.

Fruit Salad

Ask each child to bring in a piece of fruit mentioned in the story. Have a big basket available for the children to put their fruit in when they arrive at school. When it is time to make the fruit salad, each child washes and prepares the fruit that was brought.

Fruits needed for the salad:

apples

bananas

grapes

pears

The Relatives Came

Caldecott Honor Book

Cynthia Rylant
Illustrated by Stephen Gammell
Bradbury Press, 1985

This book details the excitement and activities of a family reunion. One thing most families enjoy when they get together is eating. In this book, the family eats up all the strawberries and melons. Your class will enjoy cutting and serving strawberries and watermelon. You might want to introduce several kinds of melon, in addition to watermelon.

Strawberries and Melons

strawberries

watermelon

cantaloupe

muskmelon

honeydew melon

Each child cuts the strawberries and melons and arranges them on a serving tray or in a bowl.

The Little Mouse,
the Red Ripe Strawberry,
and the Big Hungry Bear

Don and Audrey Wood
Illustrated by Don Wood
Child's Play, 1984

How would *you* hide a red, ripe, juicy strawberry from a big hungry bear?

Fresh Strawberries

If strawberries are available locally, arrange a field trip to go strawberry-picking. If this is not possible, buy them at the grocery store. Let the children carefully wash them and eat them. You might even want to have a funny-nose-and-glasses disguise to wear while you eat them. Watch out for the big hungry bear!

🐻 🐻 🐻

Curly-Locks

Traditional Mother Goose

Curly-locks, curly-locks
Wilt thou be mine?
Thou shall not wash dishes
Nor yet feed the swine;

But sit on a cushion
And sew a fine seam
And feed upon strawberries,
Sugar and cream.

Strawberries and Cream

2 – 3 pints of strawberries

2 pints heavy cream

powdered sugar

Let the children wash and slice the strawberries and put them in a bowl. Mix the cream with the strawberries and serve in individual bowls. Sprinkle with powdered sugar if desired. Sit on a cushion and enjoy!

 ðŸ‚ ðŸ‚ ðŸ‚

"Bananas and Cream" from Every Time I Climb a Tree

David McCord
Illustrated by Marc Simont
Little, Brown, and Co., 1925

In the poem book *Every Time I Climb a Tree* you will find the poem "Bananas and Cream." Like the children in the poem, all your students will yell for after hearing this poem is bananas and cream!

Bananas and Cream

For each child you will need:

1 banana

½ cup milk or cream

Let each child peel and slice the banana. Pour in the milk and enjoy.

Rain Makes Applesauce

Caldecott Honor Book

Julian Scheer
Illustrated by Marvin Bileck
Holiday House, 1964

Children love the humor in this book of silly sentences. In addition to the obvious silly sentences and detailed illustrations, please take note of the lower right-hand side of the page, where you will see a little boy and girl planting and caring for an apple tree through the four seasons. In the fall, the apples are picked and the two children make applesauce.

Applesauce

1 cooking apple per child

water

2 teaspoons cinnamon

Have the children quarter and core the apples. Be sure to remove all seeds. Put the apple pieces in a large pot. Add ½ to ¾ cup of water and cinnamon. Add water if needed as the apples cook down. Cook until apples are mushy. If you want a smoother applesauce, peel the apples before cooking or put them through a food mill after cooking.

The Old Woman Who Lived under a Hill

Traditional Mother Goose

There was an old woman
Lived under a hill
And if she's not gone
She lives there still.

Baked apples she sold
And cranberry pies,
And she's the old woman
Who never told lies.

Baked Apples

1 apple per child

cinnamon

brown sugar

whipped cream

Let the children wash and core their apples. Put the apples in a cake pan. Have each child fill his or her apple core with brown sugar. Sprinkle with cinnamon. Add enough water to cover the bottom of the cake pan. Bake for 45 minutes to an hour in a 450° oven. Serve warm with whipped cream.

Tight Times

Reading Rainbow Selection

Barbara Shook Hazen
Illustrated by Trina Schart Hyman
Viking Press, 1979

When Dad loses his job and the family goes through "tight times," they find that they have to cut back on some of the things they were used to. They eat Mr. Bulk cereal, instead of cereal in little boxes, and they go to the sprinkler instead of the beach. Instead of eating roast beef, they now have to eat "soupy things with lima beans." After reading this book, serve lima beans in class. You can buy frozen limas, or buy the dry limas and make them from scratch.

Lima Beans

12 oz. bag of dried lima beans

Sort beans and discard any that look bad. Empty the bag of beans into a large cooking pot. Cover beans with water and soak overnight. The next day, add more water if needed and bring to a boil. Turn down the heat and simmer beans in a covered pot for approximately ½ hour or until tender. Serve with butter.

Alexander and the Terrible, Horrible, No Good, Very Bad Day

Reading Rainbow Selection

Judith Viorst
Illustrated by Ray Cruz
Atheneum, 1984

On this terrible day, nothing goes right for poor Alexander. There's kissing on TV, and he hates kissing. There's lima beans for dinner, and he hates lima beans. When children help prepare food, they will usually taste what they cook. They may surprise you—and even themselves—by *liking* lima beans!

Lima Beans

If you want to cook dried lima beans, refer to the recipe listed under the book *Tight Times* on page 110. If you prefer a quicker method, buy a bag of frozen beans and cook according to the directions on the bag.

When I Was Young in the Mountains

Caldecott Honor Book
Reading Rainbow Selection

Cynthia Rylant
Illustrated by Diane Goode
E. P. Dutton, 1982

This is a delightful book about earlier times and life in the mountains. Your students can compare shopping at a general store, baptisms in the river, and using a "johnny-house" at night to lifestyles we are accustomed to today.

Okra

Many children have never tasted okra. You can buy it frozen at the grocery store if you cannot find it fresh.

Wash three or four okra; cut off stems. Slice into 1" pieces and put into ½ to ¾ cup boiling water. Turn down the heat and simmer until tender. Drain off water. Salt and pepper to taste and butter if desired.

The Enormous Turnip

Traditional Fairy Tale

In this fairy tale, a farmer grows an *enormous* turnip. It is so large that he needs the help of his wife, a little girl, a little boy, and several animals to pull it up!

Many children have never tasted turnips before and it is surprising the number of children who will ask for seconds.

Turnips

You will need about 1 pound of fresh turnips. Peel the waxy skin off the turnips. Cut into 1" cubes. Put them into a pot and cover with water. Boil turnips 8 to 10 minutes or until tender. Salt and pepper to taste. Serve with butter.

ع. ع. ع.

The Carrot Seed

Ruth Krauss
Harper, 1945

When a little boy plants a carrot seed, he is undaunted by all the members of his family who tell him it will never grow.

Carrots

You will need one carrot per child. Have each child scrub and scrape a carrot, then slice the carrot and put half the carrot slices in a bowl and half in a cooking pot. Boil or steam the carrots until tender. The children can taste and compare the raw and cooked carrots. You can also bring a carrot with the green top still attached to show the children what carrots look like when they grow.

Scrambled Eggs Super!

Dr. Seuss
Random House, 1953

Peter T. Hooper gathers hundreds of eggs from hundreds of very unusual birds to make Scrambled eggs Super–dee–Dooper–dee–Booper, Special deluxe–a–la Peter T. Hooper. To make your scrambled eggs Super–dee–Dooper, add onions, green peppers, cheese and ham.

Special Deluxe Scrambled Eggs

1 egg per child

⅓ cup milk

1 tablespoon butter

4 oz. cheddar cheese, grated

1 onion, diced

1 green pepper, diced

1 pkg. ham, cubed

Let the children grate the cheese and cut up the ham and vegetables. Have each child crack and mix his or her own egg and put it into a large mixing bowl. Add milk. Melt butter in skillet. Saute onions and green peppers until tender. Add eggs and cook until set, adding cheese at the last minute.

Green Eggs and Ham

Dr. Seuss
Random House, 1960

Do you like green eggs and ham? Try them and you may, I say.

Green Eggs and Ham

1 egg per child
green food coloring
1 pkg. sliced ham
1 tablespoon butter or margarine

Allow each child to crack his or her egg into a small bowl. Add a drop or two of green food coloring and scramble it up well. Add this egg to a larger bowl that will hold all eggs to be cooked. Cut the sliced ham into half-inch squares.

Melt the butter in an electric skillet. Add eggs and cook. When eggs are just about set, add the diced ham pieces.

"Would you eat them in a car?"

The Man Who Tried to Save Time

Phyllis Krasilovsky
Illustrated by Marcia Sewell
Doubleday, 1979

Once there was a man who lived in a little house with his cat. He cleaned his house, tended his garden, and went to the office on a regular schedule every day. One day he decides to sit in his rocking chair all day instead of doing his daily duties. He tries to save time by doing his duties faster, so he will have more time to just sit and rock. He eats his breakfast before going to bed and goes to sleep with his clothes on so he can save time in the morning. After a while he realizes that he likes his old way best. He returns to his regular schedule, which, among other things, includes eating his breakfast of orange juice, toast, and eggs in the morning.

Orange Juice, Toast, and Eggs

Divide your class into three groups. The first group makes orange juice from frozen concentrate, or squeezes oranges for fresh juice. The second group makes and butters a piece of toast for each child. And the third group cracks, cooks, and serves one scrambled egg per student.

Gregory the Terrible Eater

Reading Rainbow Selection

Mitchell Sharmat
Illustrated by Jose Aruego and Ariane Dewey
Scholastic Book Services, 1980

Gregory is a goat and his parents are concerned about his eating habits. They think he should eat good foods like tin cans and the evening newspaper, instead of junk food like fruits, vegetables, and eggs. Finally they compromise and Gregory agrees to eat scrambled eggs, orange juice, and a piece of waxed paper. Even though Gregory's parents wouldn't let him skip the waxed paper, you might wish to allow your students to!

Scrambled Eggs

Let each child crack an egg and scramble it in a small bowl. Many children have never had the opportunity to crack their own egg and this is an important part of cooking this recipe. After scrambling their individual egg, let them pour it in a large bowl. Add ¼ to ½ cup of milk to the egg mixture. Melt 2 tablespoons of butter in an electric skillet and scramble eggs until they are set. Serve each child an egg and a glass of orange juice.

Fresh-Squeezed Orange Juice

Instead of using frozen orange juice or cartons of orange juice, you might want to make fresh-squeezed juice with your students.

Each child should bring an orange to school. Roll the orange on the table or other hard surface before cutting. This helps to make your orange juicier for squeezing. Each child cuts his or her orange in half, and, using a manual or electric juicer, squeezes the orange for juice.

Little Miss Muffet

Traditional Mother Goose

Little Miss Muffet
Sat on a tuffet,
Eating her curds and whey.
Along came a spider
And sat down beside her,
And frightened Miss Muffet away.

Curds and Whey

2 cups milk

salt

1½ tablespoons vinegar

Heat the milk until it just starts to boil. Remove from heat. Add vinegar and stir constantly until curds start to form. Separate the curds from the liquid. This liquid is the whey. Taste a small amount of curds on bread or your favorite cracker. Add a pinch of salt if desired.

Peanut Butter and Jelly

Illustrated by Nadine Bernard Westcott
E. P. Dutton, 1987

A version of this play rhyme is also a song. It is a humorous song about making peanut butter and jelly. The recipe below is for making peanut butter. If you also wish to make jelly, see the recipe on page 38 for *Blueberries for Sal*.

Peanut Butter

1 jar or bag of shelled peanuts
cooking oil

Place ¼ cup of peanuts in a blender at a time. Turn blender on high and blend for 10 to 15 seconds. If the peanuts need to be crushed more, repeat for 10 to 15 more seconds. This keeps the motor from overworking. When blended, add another ¼ cup of peanuts to the blender. Add a little oil if it looks like the peanut butter is dry. Some peanuts are very oily and you do not need much oil. Other peanuts are drier and more oil will be needed. Add enough oil to moisten the peanut butter to a spreadable consistency.

The Vanishing Pumpkin

Tony Johnson
Illustrated by Tomie dePaola
G. P. Putnam's Sons, 1983

A 700-year-old woman and an 800-year-old man went as fast as they could—"in fact they fairly flew"—in search of the pumpkin that was snitched from their garden. Many children do not realize that pumpkin for their pumpkin pies does not just come out of a can. Cook a pumpkin to taste or to use in a pumpkin pie recipe.

Cooked Pumpkin

Be sure you buy a *cooking* pumpkin and not a pumpkin grown strictly for decorating purposes. Cut open the pumpkin and clean out all the seeds and strings. Cut the shell of the pumpkin into pieces. Steam the pumpkin pieces by placing them in a steamer or metal strainer. Put the steamer on the bottom of a large pot and add water just to the bottom of the steamer. Steam the pieces in a covered pot for 30 to 45 minutes or until pumpkin is soft. Peel the rind from the pumpkin pulp. Put pumpkin pulp through a food mill or blender until smooth. Use as you would canned pumpkin.

The Very Hungry Caterpillar

Eric Carle
Philomel, 1983

The very hungry caterpillar eats his way through lots of food before growing into a beautiful butterfly. Have each child in class bring one or two of these foods to cut into bite-sized pieces for the class to enjoy:

apples	*salami*
strawberries	*lollipops*
pears	*cherry pie*
plums	*oranges*
chocolate cake	*sausages*
ice cream cones	*cupcakes*
pickles	*watermelons*
Swiss cheese	

Sylvester and the Magic Pebble

Caldecott Award Winner

William Steig
Simon and Schuster, 1969

Sylvester finds a red, round magic pebble and discovers his wishes all come true. When he is frightened by a lion he wishes, without thinking, that he was a rock. Will he ever get changed back into a donkey?

Alfalfa Sandwiches

On a picnic while looking for Sylvester, his parents have some alfalfa sandwiches. You can buy alfalfa sprouts in the produce section of the grocery store or you can grow your own. Alfalfa sprouts are easy to grow. Buy alfalfa seeds at a health food store. Put 1 tablespoon of seeds in a mayonnaise jar. Cut 4 or 5 pieces of cheesecloth large enough to fit over the top of the jar. Secure the cheesecloth pieces over the opening of the jar with a rubber band. Run water in the jar and drain through the cheesecloth. Rinse the seeds daily and keep the jar in the sun. They should sprout in about five to seven days.

Make sandwiches by placing a small bunch of sprouts and a tablespoon of plain yogurt in a half piece of pita or pocket bread.

What a Good Lunch!

Shigeo Wantanabe
Illustrated by Yasuo Ohotomo
Philomel, 1978

Little bear is learning how to eat properly with humorous results. Your class will enjoy fixing and eating this well-balanced meal. Since there are several courses to this meal, convenience foods are suggested. If you wish to make any of these courses using fresh ingredients or from scratch, recipes appear in other areas of this book for all of these foods.

Your lunch should include:

- Cream of Chicken Soup: 2 to 4 cans of commercially prepared soup.
- Bread with Butter and Strawberry Jam: Each child prepares his or her slice.
- Spaghetti: 1 pound of spaghetti and 2 jars of commercial spaghetti sauce.
- Salad: Each child can bring an item to prepare and put into the salad, including carrots, lettuce, celery, and cucumbers.

Banbury Fair

Traditional Mother Goose

As I was going to Banbury,
Upon a summer's day,
My dame had butter, eggs, and fruit,
And I had corn and hay,

Jack drove the ox, and Tom the swine,
Dick took the foal and mare;
I sold them all—then home to dine
From famous Banbury fair.

Homemade Butter

See the recipe on page 34 for the book *Pancakes for Breakfast*.

Eggs

You will need 1 egg per child. Put the eggs in a large pot and cover them completely with water. Boil 12 to 15 minutes.

Fruit

Have several kinds of fruit available for the children to sample, or mix them all together for a fruit salad. Some fruits to try include:

apples	*pears*
bananas	*pineapple*
kiwi	*grapes*
oranges	*cantaloupe*
muskmelon	*watermelon*
honeydew melon	

King Bidgood's in the Bathtub

Caldecott Honor Book

Audrey Wood
Illustrated by Don Wood
Harcourt Brace Jovanovich, 1985

Everyone tries to think of a way to get the king to come out of the tub. But "King Bidgood's in the bathtub and he won't come out!" Will *you* know what to do?

Lunch in the Tub

The king has a feast in the tub. Though you might not want to cook up all he has eaten, you may want to serve cookies or lunch in a cardboard bathtub for your students to re-enact this story.

Teachers might want to send home a note suggesting this book and activity for the children to do at home. Maybe mom or dad will serve them lunch in the real bathtub at home!

Teddy Bear's Picnic

Jimmy Kennedy
Illustrated by Alexander Day
Green Tiger Press, 1983

This book beautifully illustrates the song of the same name. Ask your students to invite their teddy bears and bring a sack lunch to school. Take a walk and spread your picnic blankets on the grass to enjoy your lunches. You might also want to play the record that comes with the book before, after, or during your picnic. Oh, and you might also want to go in disguise!

Teddy Bear Picnic

Instead of having sack lunches, your students might wish to take along the food that the teddy bears enjoyed in the book. The illustrations show the bears dining on:

sweet corn

sandwiches

celery

potato chips

cake

fruit

Picnic

Emily Arnold McCully
Harper and Row, 1984

A mouse family goes on a picnic in this wordless book, but the baby mouse gets lost on the way. If you plan to take your class on a similar picnic, be sure you do not lose any classmates!

Picnic

Pack up a picnic basket and a red and white checked tablecloth and take your class on a picnic. You can enjoy some of the same foods that the mouse family did:

watermelon

sandwiches

milk

cheese

orange juice

baked beans

sausage

Maybe you will be lucky and find some wild raspberries to eat, just like baby mouse did!

Popcorn

Frank Asch
Parents' Press, 1979

When Sam's parents go to a Halloween party, Sam invites some friends over for his own party. Every friend that arrives brings some popcorn. Sam and his friends decide to pop *all* the popcorn in one pot and before they know it there is popcorn to the rooftop! When Sam's parents come home, they bring a surprise for Sam—more popcorn! Though you will probably not want to pop a full pound of popcorn, you will need to make a lot.

Popcorn

For an experience much like the book and one your children will never forget, place a sheet in the center of the room and put a popcorn popper in the middle of the sheet. Making sure your children are standing back from the sheet, pop your popcorn without a lid on your popper. Though the popcorn will probably not fill the school to the roof, it will pop all over the room.

Let your students enjoy the popcorn that landed on the clean sheet. You might want to do this at your next Halloween party!

The Popcorn Book

Tomie dePaola
Scholastic Book Services, 1978

This book gives some interesting facts about America's favorite snack food. Did you know that colonists even ate popcorn for breakfast? They ate popcorn with cream much like we eat cereal. After reading this book with your class, why not try a bowl of popcorn with cream or milk?

Popcorn with Cream

Pop your popcorn in a popcorn popper, or in a pan on the stove. If you can, make popcorn in a fireplace or build a campfire and make popcorn using a fireplace popper. If you have access to a microwave, you might want to compare making popcorn this way with the ways that the corn is popped in the book. Included in the book are two additional ways to pop corn that you might also want to choose.

Whichever way you choose to pop it, provide bowls, milk, and maybe a little sugar and try eating your popcorn like the colonists liked to eat it!

The Seasons of Arnold's Apple Tree

Gail Gibbons
Holiday House, 1984

Arnold has a secret place under an apple tree. He watches it change through all the seasons. In the fall he gathers the apples and makes apple pie and apple cider. Recipes for both of these are included in the book. In the winter he strings popcorn and berries to hang on the tree branches to feed the birds. You might want to make the apple pie and cider using the recipes in the book or you may want to feed the animals in the winter.

Popcorn and Berries

Pop popcorn the day before you want to string it. It is much easier to string day-old popcorn than freshly popped. Using a needle and long thread, string the popcorn and berries. Hang from a tree near your windows and see how many birds come to feast. If you do this, please continue to feed the birds throughout the winter once you start, as they will become dependent on your feedings.

A Treasury of Flannelboard Stories

by Jeanette Graham Bay

There is nothing like a good story to captivate a young child, and this new collection offers twenty-one original flannelboard stories by a master storyteller and teacher. The flannelboard is an exceptionally good medium because it can involve children in the activity by cutting out and coloring the patterns, moving the characters on the board, and acting out the roles in the story. This can bring out a child's creativity and imagination.

These stories were written for children from preschool to the third grade, and they were specifically developed for the flannelboard. They include adventure, fantasy, nature, suspense, problem solving, dinosaurs, a visit the library, and many other delightful topics. Each story comes complete with an easy-to-use script and full-size patterns for all the characters and elements. Simply photocopy and color them, paste them to flannel or Velcro®, and cut them out. The characters can be used again and again with other stories the children may create.

In her introduction the author offers valuable suggestions that will further enhance the use of these stories in the classroom, library and at home. She has added an annotated list of recommended books and other resources for teachers, librarians, storytellers and parents.

Jeanette Graham Bay has been a preschool teacher for over thirty years, entertaining and educating generations of children with her storytelling skills and her rich repertoire. She is the author of *The Alleyside Book of Flannelboard Stories*, and she resides in Macedon, New York.

Sassafras Holmes and the Library Mysteries

By Carolmarie Stock

Illustrated by Anne Hershenburgh

Youngsters often find the library a mysterious place—a place where great treasures remain hidden just out of their reach and a place with many strange rules and customs. But here at last is a most delightful way to help young readers unravel the mysteries of the library! Through the adventures of young detective Sassafras Holmes and her friend Jane Watson, elementary students will eagerly learn about the Dewey Decimal System, using reference materials, and the importance of reading, as well as valuable lessons on library manners and book care. Younger children will sit spellbound as you spin each of the eight complete Sassafras Holmes yarns; older students will enjoy reading the stories for themselves in the illustrated, easy-to-read format. It's elementary!

Carolmarie Stock is a professional storyteller and middle school librarian and has worked in both the Chicago and Cincinnati areas. She has also served as associate producer of a live television talk show and is active in community theatre. A published poet, Ms. Stock is currently working on several children's books, including a collection of fairy tales retold for the 1990s. She resides in the Cincinnati area with her teenage daughter.

Anne Hershenburgh is a talented and versatile artist noted especially for her figures, still lifes, and whimsical Victorian children. She worked for many years in the Art Department of Warner Brothers Studios, and her paintings have gained a devoted following throughout the United States and Europe.

Pardon Me, But Your References
Are Showing!

by Teddy Meister

Looking for a simple, effective, and fun way to teach reference skills? *Pardon Me, But Your References Are Showing!* contains 28 ready-to-use learning units and activities, each one designed not only to teach research, but to pique young learners' curiosity and allow them a creative, hands-on outlet for their new skills. This book is flexible enough for use as independent work, small-group cooperative learning, total class studies, or enrichment homework, with applications for whole-language and thinking skills. Topics are consistent and appropriate for curriculum enhancement at the elementary and middle-school levels in all academic areas. Each section or topic is self-explanatory and self-contained, and each is designed to quickly build youngsters' skills and confidence. Stop making reference skills a chore—start training young "research detectives" with *Pardon Me, But Your References Are Showing!*

Teddy Meister has been a classroom teacher for over 20 years, and is currently a Curriculum Resource Teacher working with administration and teachers in an Orange County, Florida, elementary school. She has published numerous professional articles and twelve books; *Pardon Me, But Your References Are Showing!* is her first book for Alleyside Press.

Children Becoming Independent Readers

The Teacher's Guide to Using
Literature-Based Reading
in the Classroom

by Tom Davidson, Ed.D.

Are you just teaching "how to read?" Or are you interested in training children to *become readers?* If you understand the difference, and if the latter idea appeals to you, you've come to the right place! *Children Becoming Independent Readers* will lead you step-by-step through the process of creating and implementing a classroom-based Independent Reading Program that will actually get kids to *want* to read. Everything you need to know is here—from creating a promotional campaign that will ensure your program's success, to building an extensive classroom library at little or no cost, to evaluating your students' success. Every step of the process is detailed with outlines, plans, and goals that you can achieve with little time and even less money—but the complete program works, and works so effectively that you'll be amazed! Stop teaching "how to read" today—and start *creating readers!*

Tom Davidson spent six years as an elementary teacher in California and Arizona and has been associated with the Education Department of West Georgia College since 1971. Currently a full Professor of Education, he has published and lectured extensively on teaching reading, language arts, preadolescent literature, and ways to stimulate independent reading in children. His first Alleyside Press book, *Share It If You Read It*, was published in 1985.